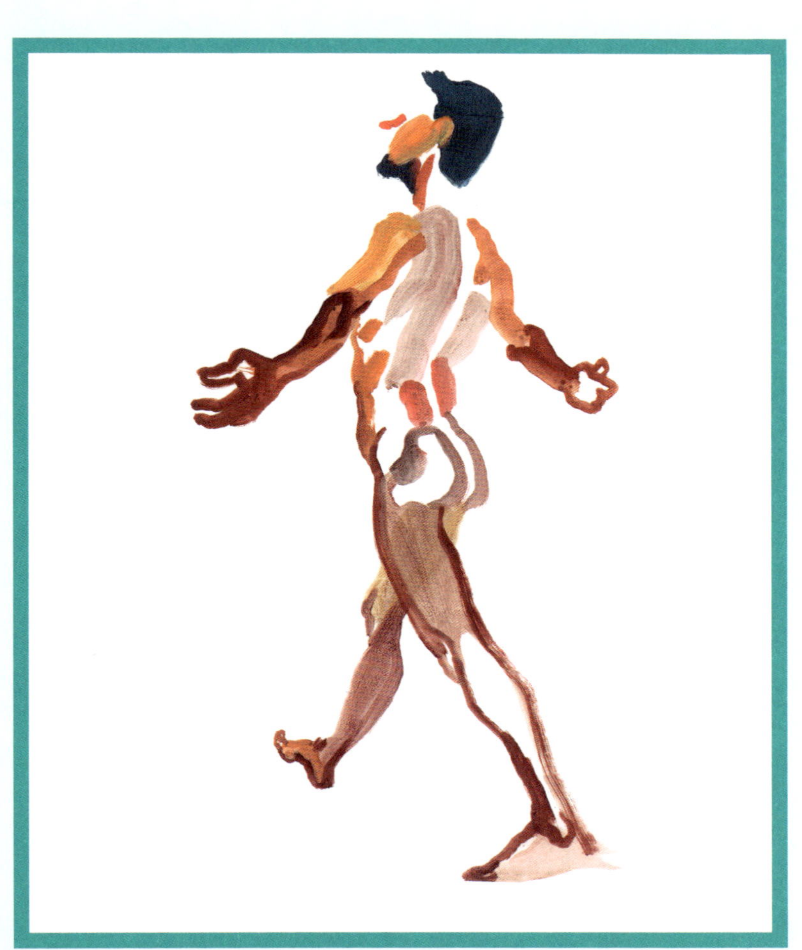

Hello World

The body speaks
in the drawings
of men by
JAMES
MCMULLAN

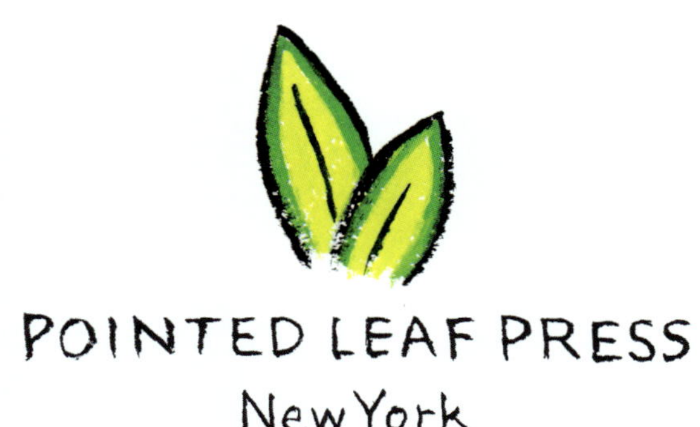

POINTED LEAF PRESS

New York

Dedication

This book is dedicated to all the men who inspired me with the creative energy of their bodies, particularly Thomas Welsh-Huggins whose extraordinary poses fueled some of my most dramatic drawings.

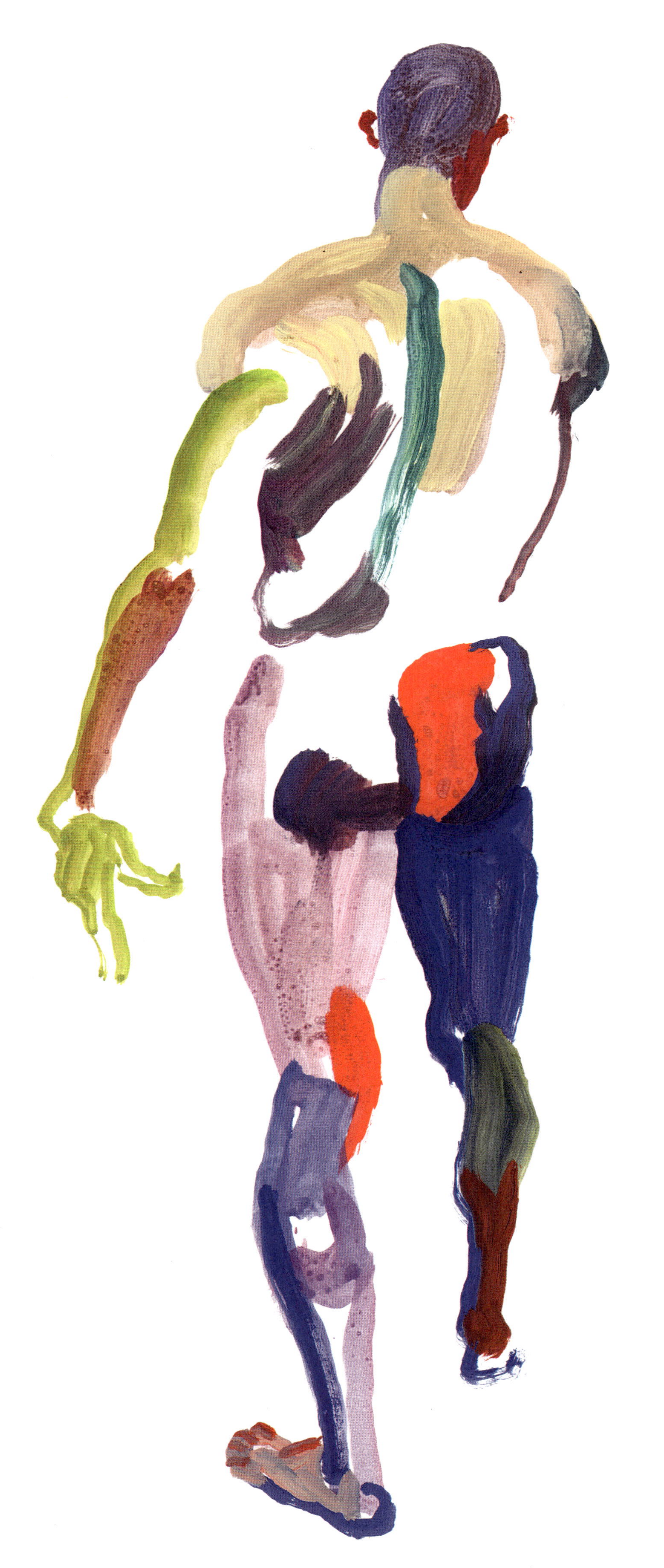

Introduction

The model steps up onto
the modelling stand—
Are his lips pursed or is
his mouth relaxed?
What is most beautiful to me—
the way he turns with
a kind of easy grace
or his remarkable legs?
Does his posture shout out
"I'm feeling pumped!"
or does it give me a whispered
"I have issues"?
I begin. Where in his body
does everything get going?
What leads the twist?
I choose the spine and make
a purple line—color feels right.
That first line sets off an
explosion of feelings and logic—
seven minutes of letting
the thoughts flow,
dipping my brush in a color,
making line after line to
build the body-poem I am
discovering.

Come on brush.
Give me flowing washes to get
that flexibility in his back.
His belly is really stretched out.
Nail that point in the ribcage
that pulls it.
I need a patch of pushy green for
the thrusting neck that seems
to be telling the head
what to think.
One choice after another
impelled by a vision of spirit
rather than muscle and bone.
The tension, beauty, difficulty,
gracefulness, fluidity, sexuality
that open my mind and my hand
to this man standing in front of me
in all his challenging reality.

what is his body saying?
what am I thinking?

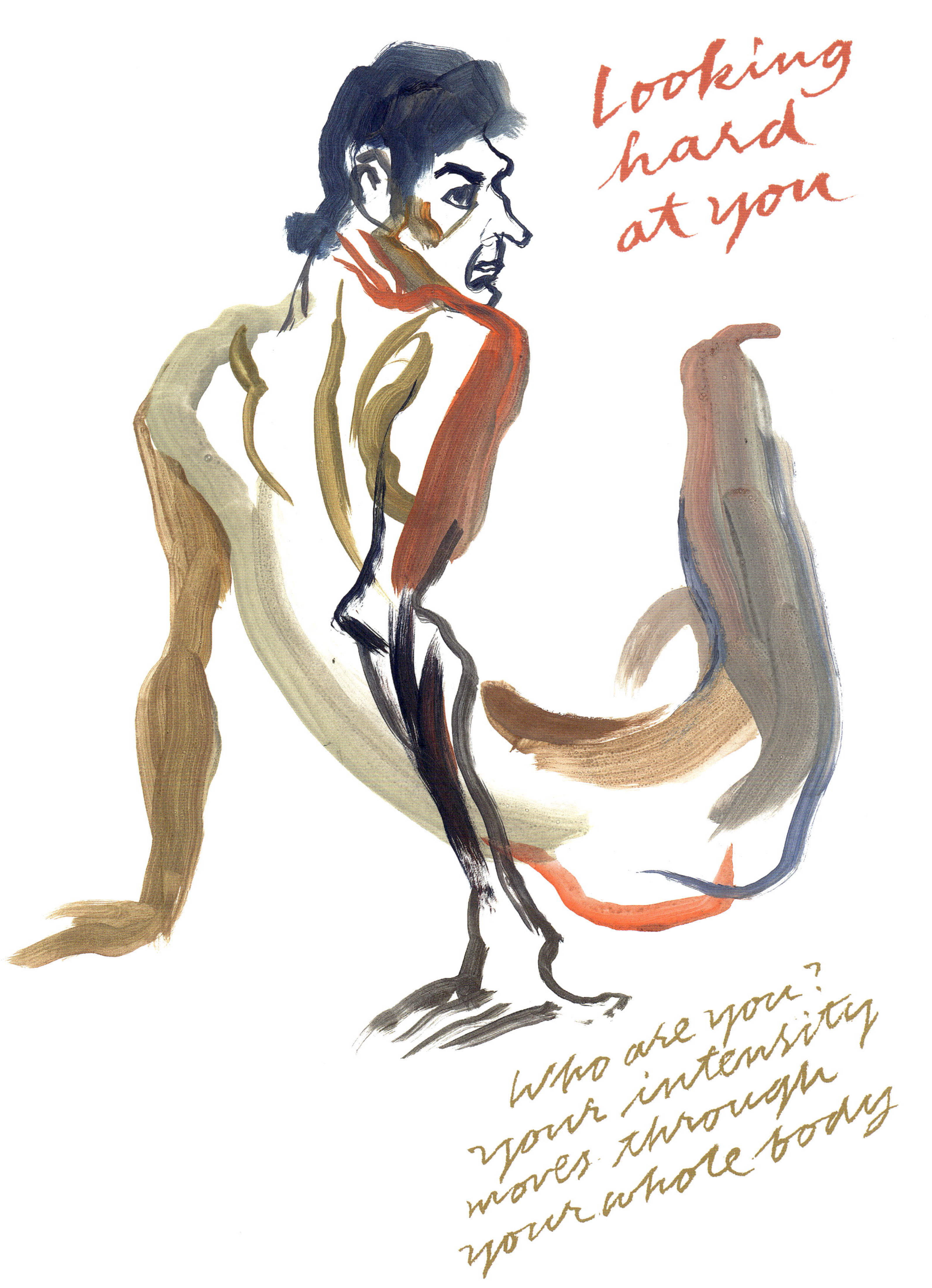

looking
hard
at you
who are you?
your intensity
moves through
your whole body

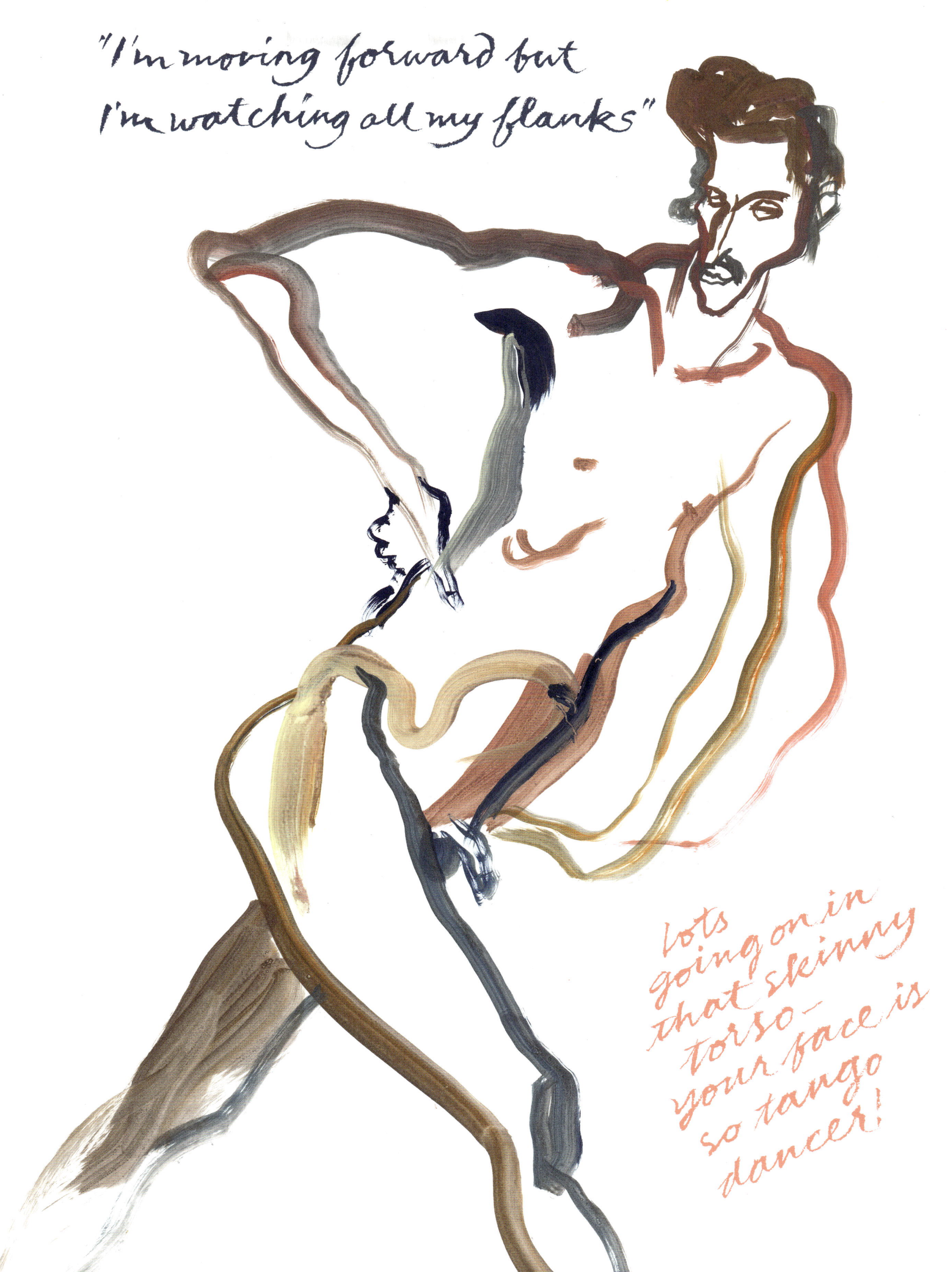
"I'm moving forward but I'm watching all my flanks"
Lots going on in that skinny torso— your face is so tango dancer!

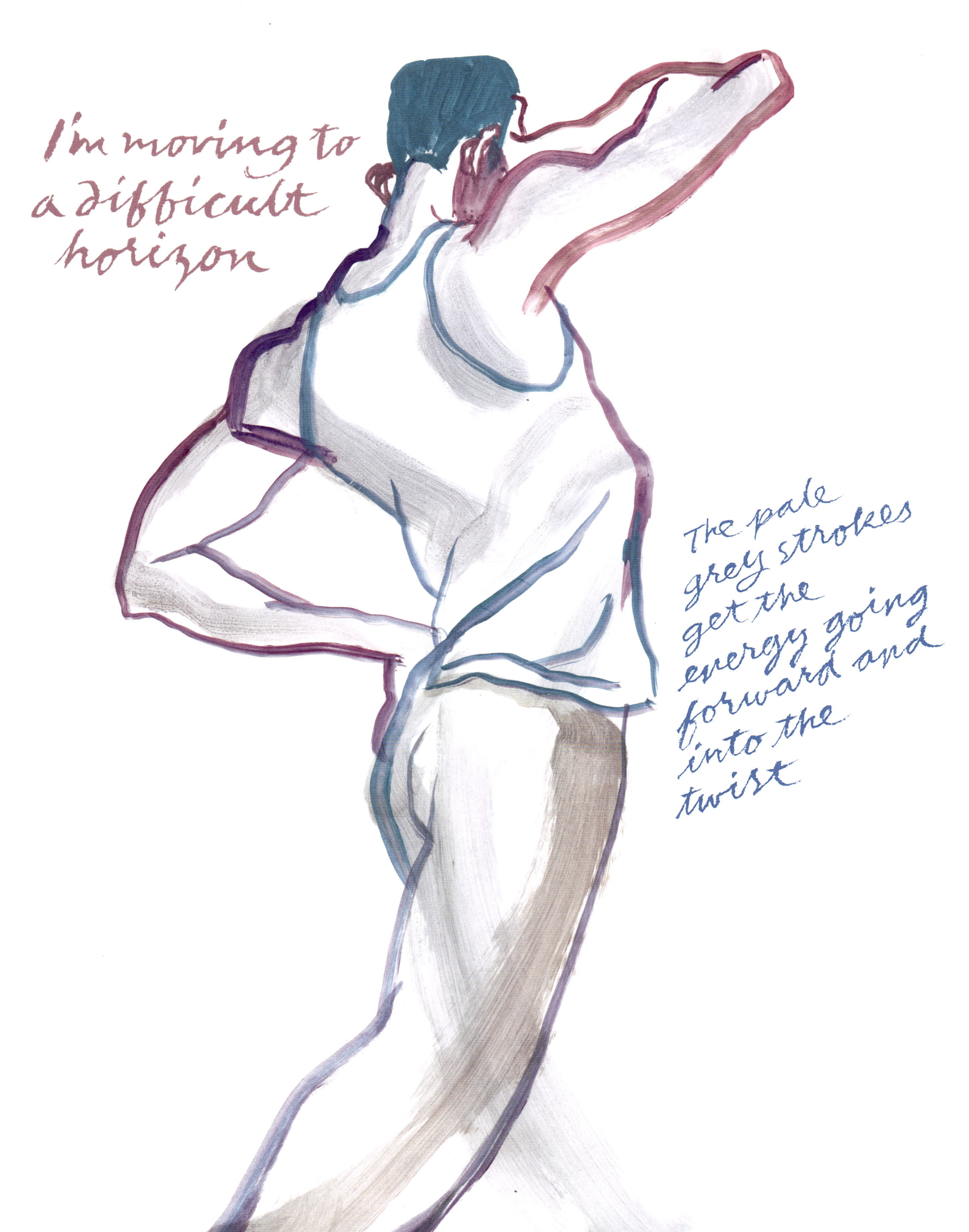
I'm moving to
a difficult
horizon

The pale
grey strokes
get the
energy going
forward and
into the
twist

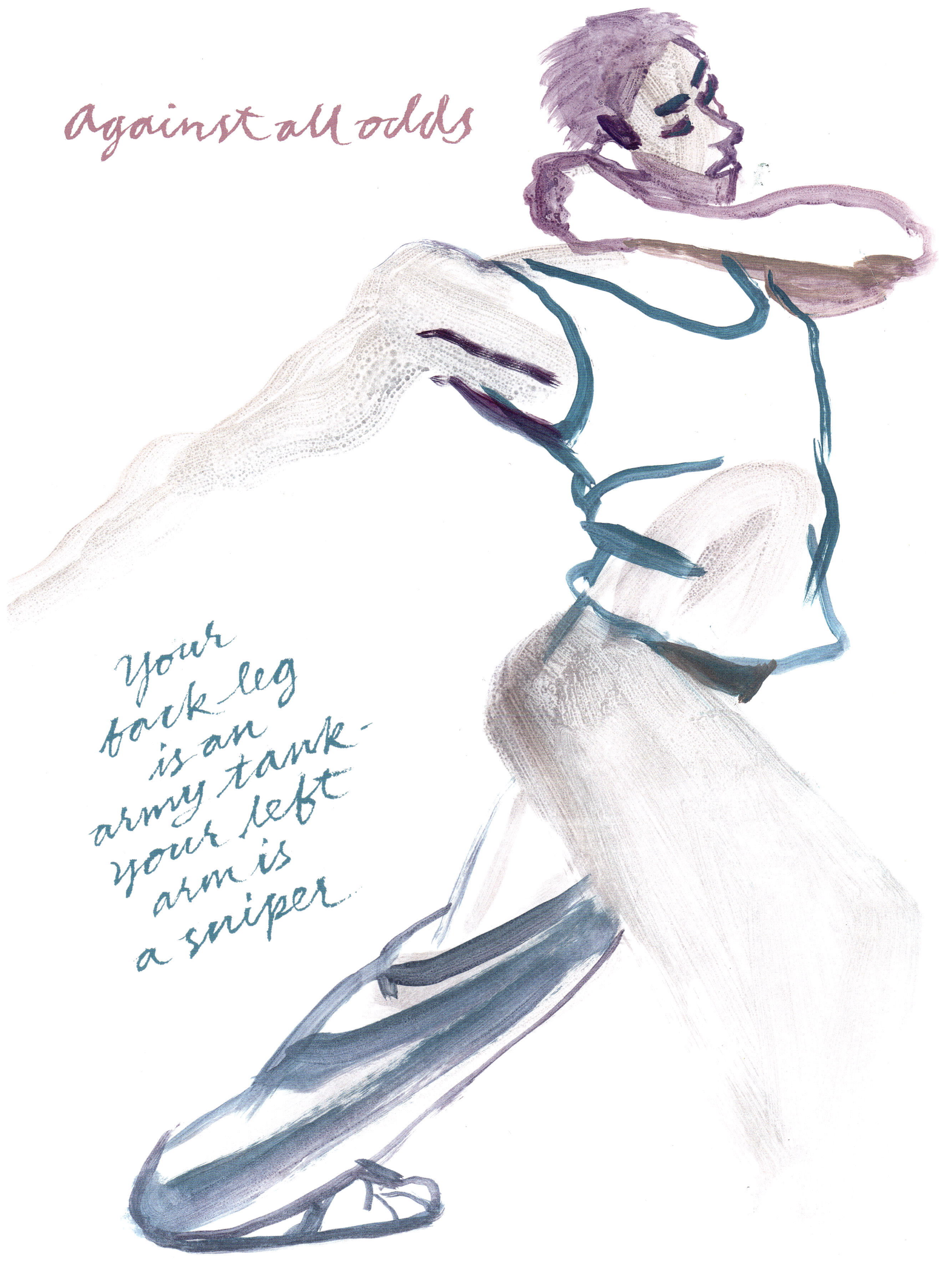
against all odds
your back leg is an army tank- your left arm is a sniper.

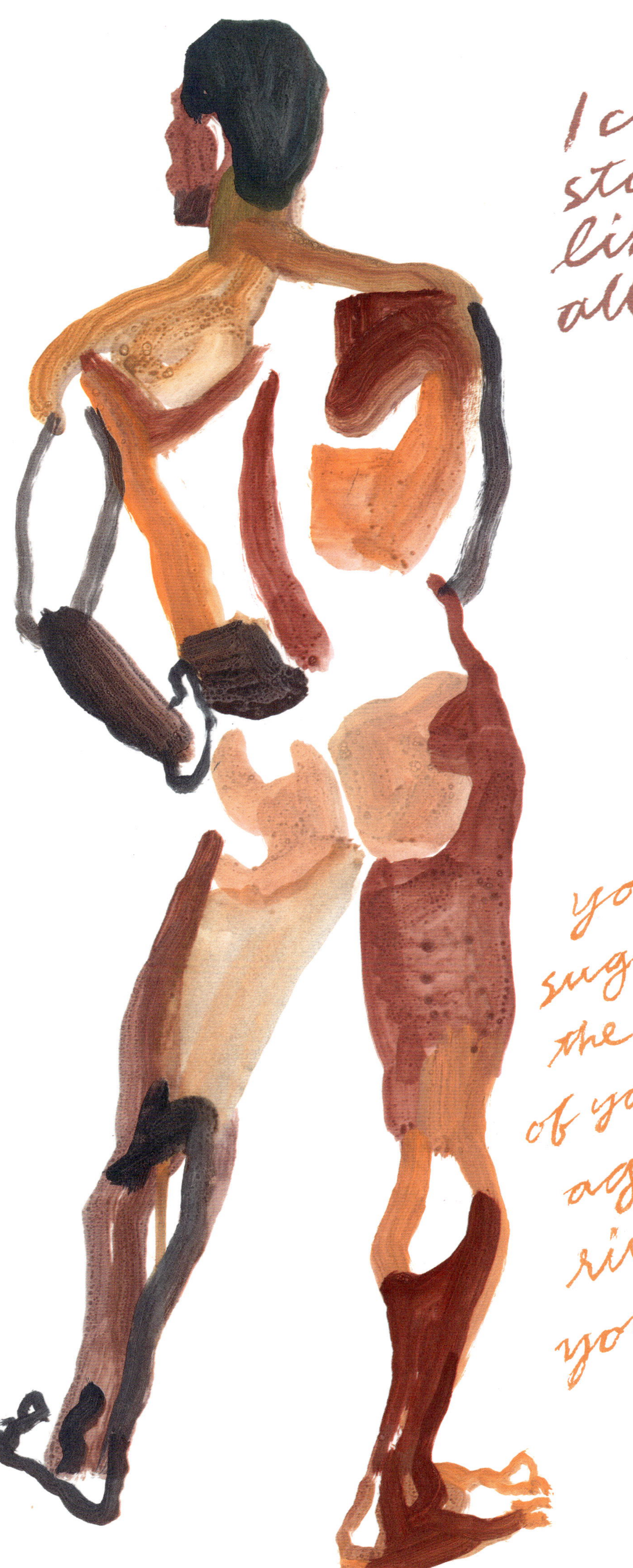

I could
stand
like this
all day

your balance
suggests a map—
the continents
of your shoulders
against the
river of
your spine

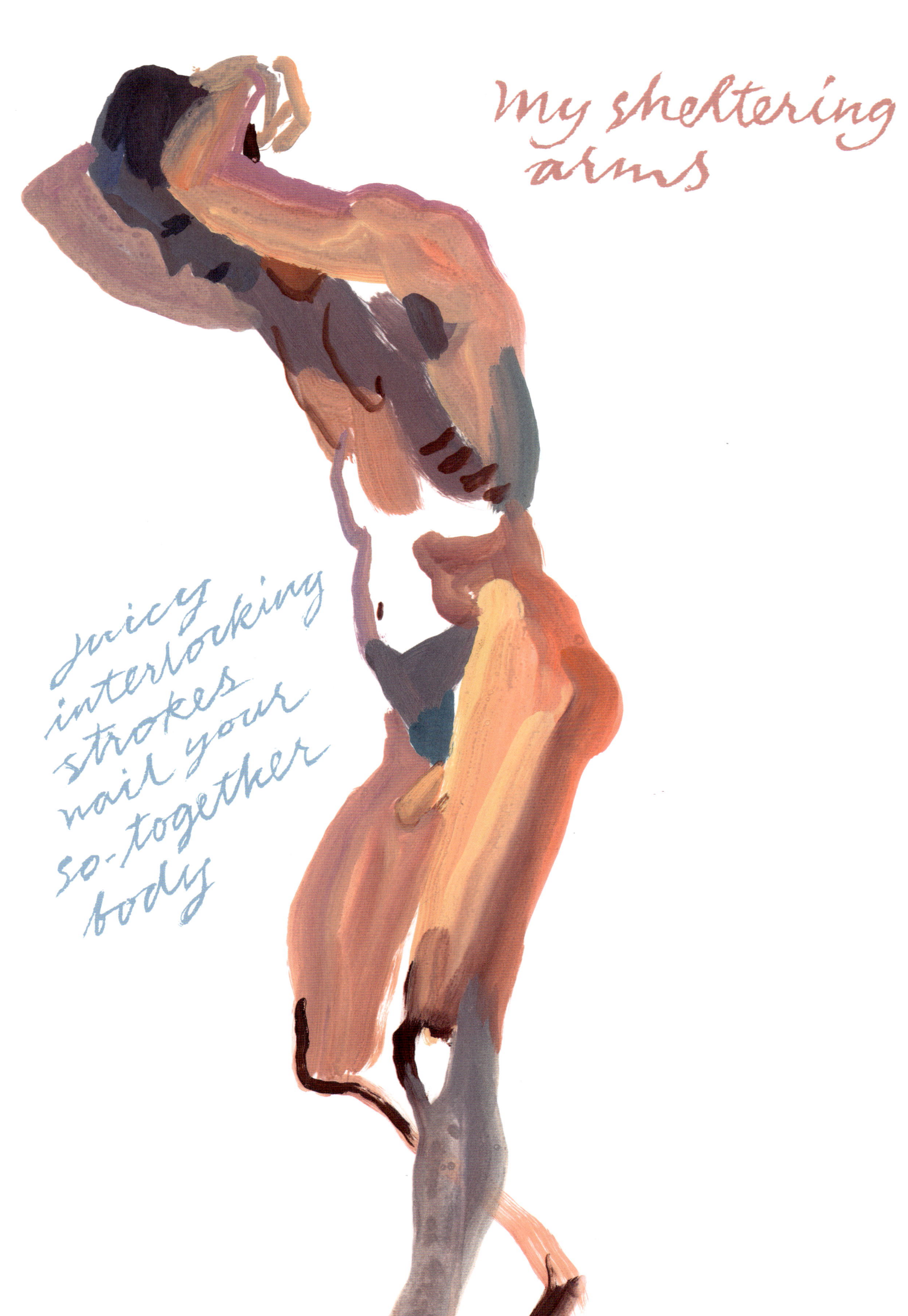

my sheltering
arms

juicy
interlocking
strokes
nail your
so-together
body

my eyes lead the stretch

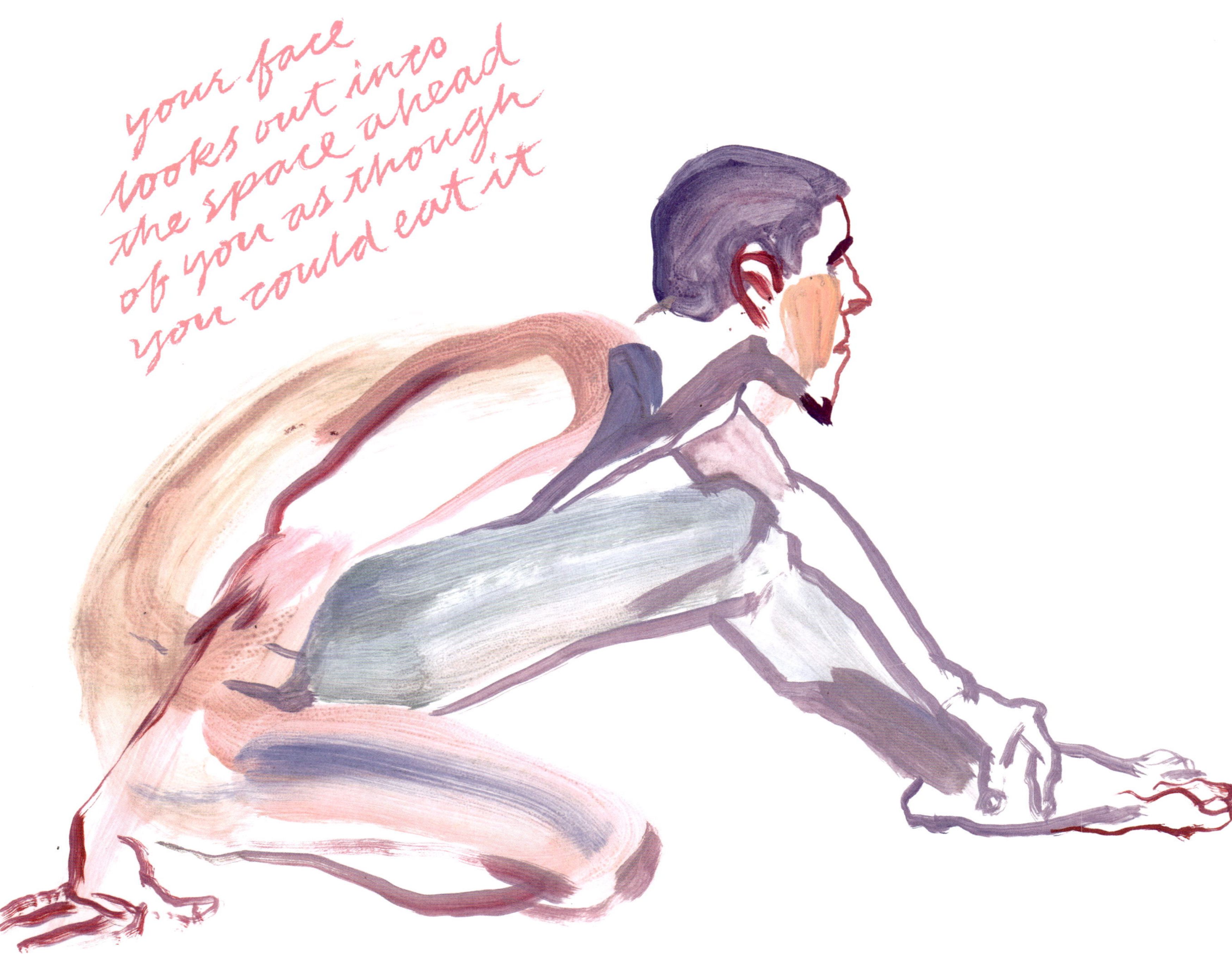

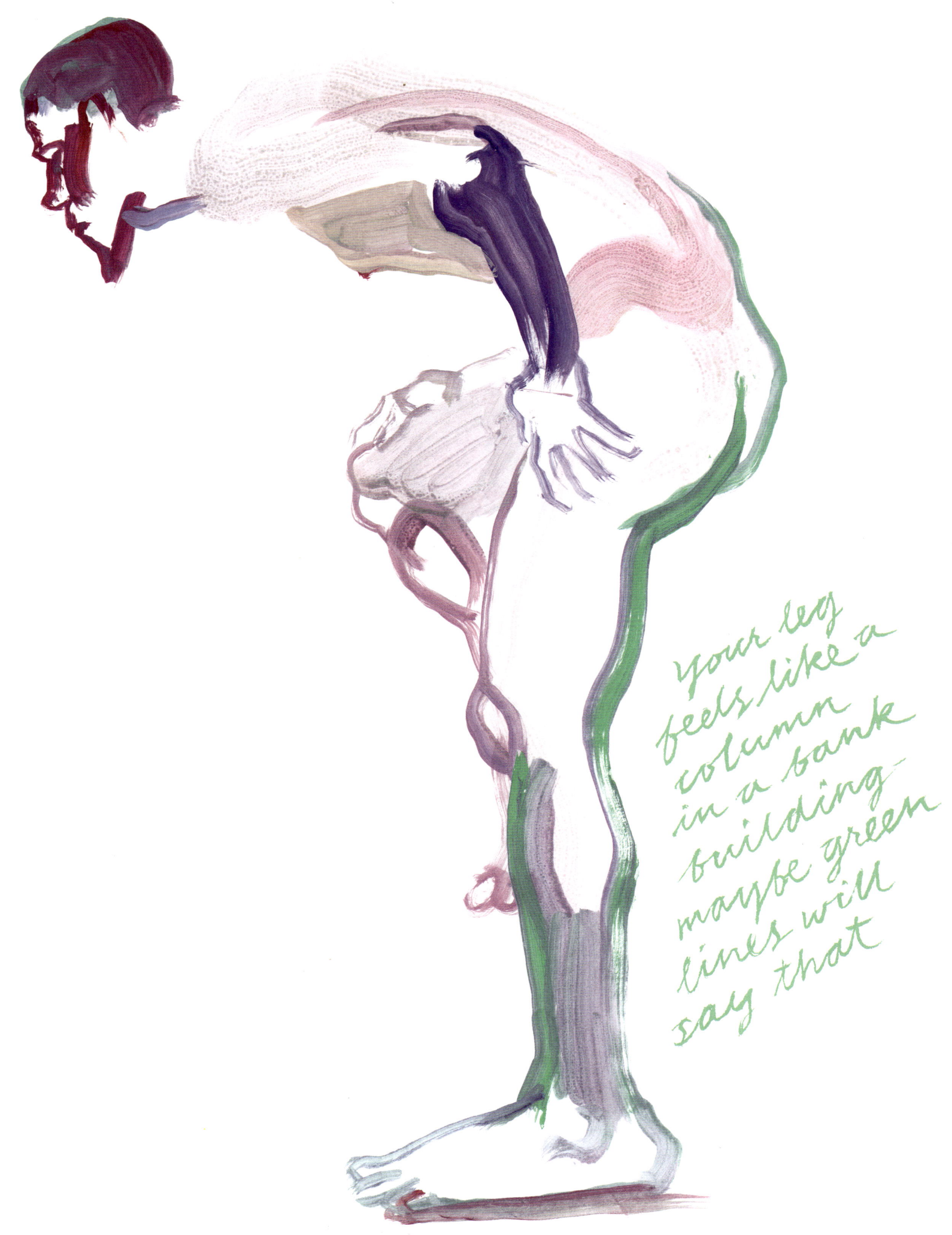

Balance like a stork
your leg
feels like a
column
in a bank
building
maybe green
lines will
say that

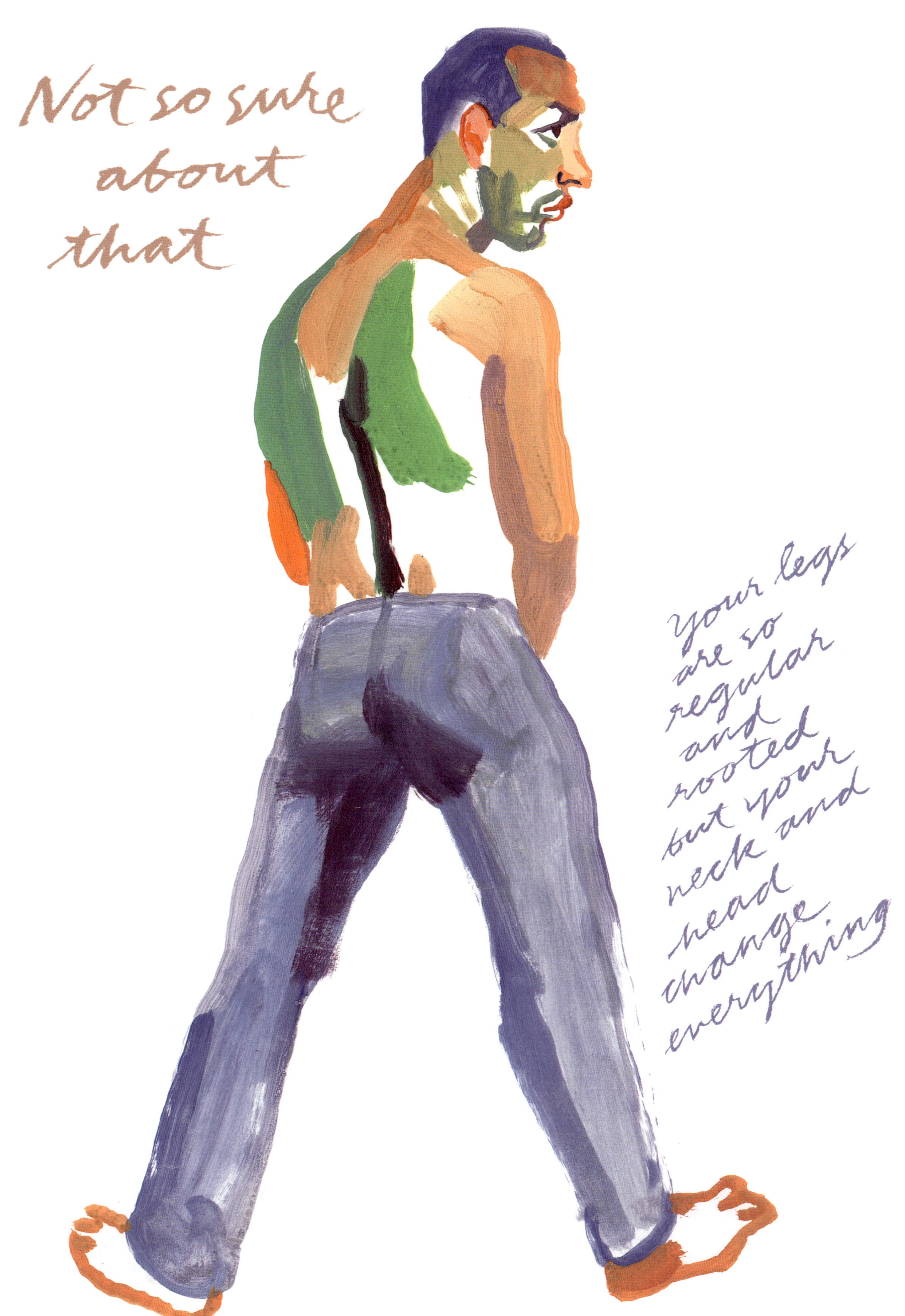

Not so sure about that

your legs are so regular and rooted but your neck and head change everything

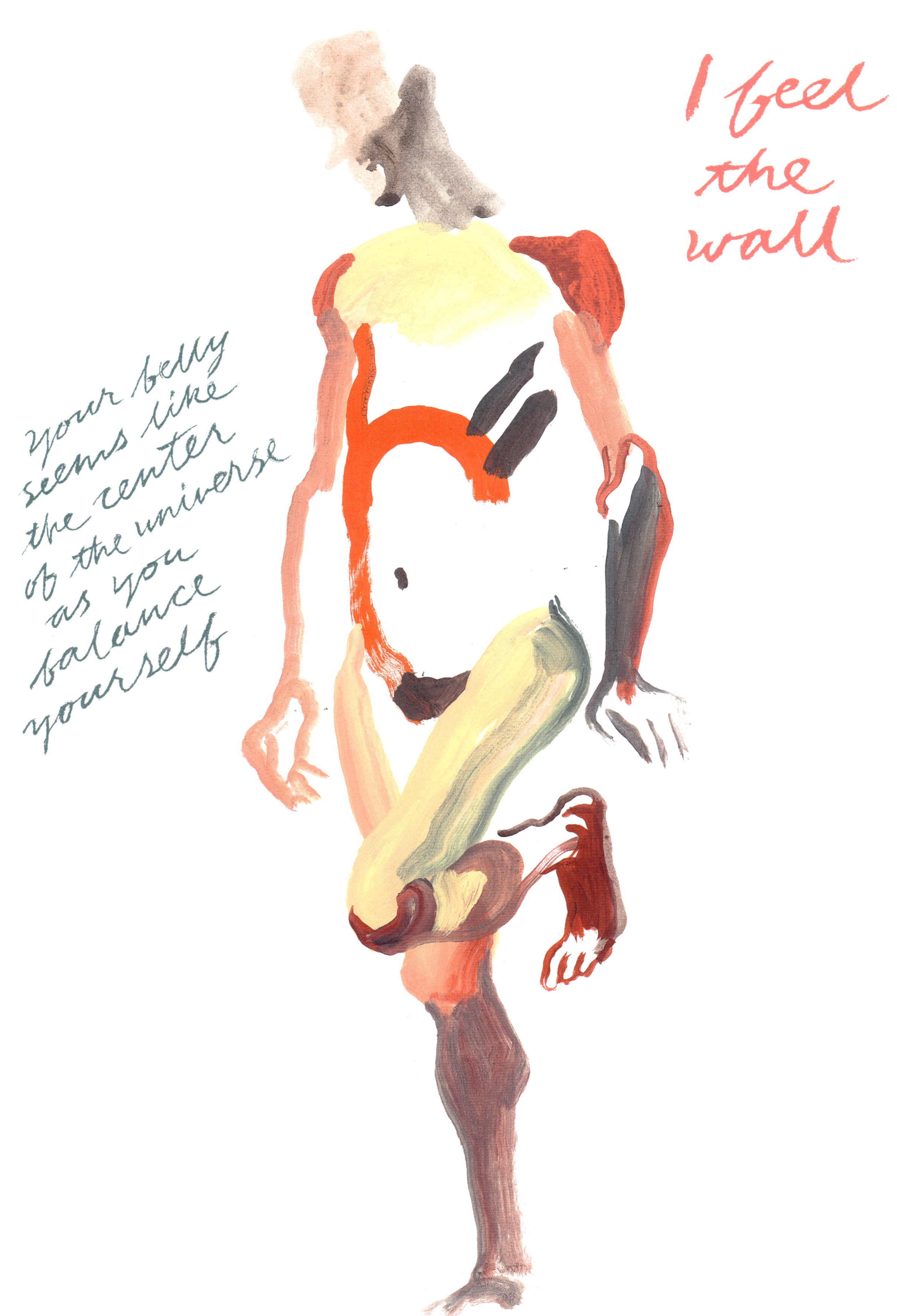

I feel
the
wall

your belly
seems like
the center
of the universe
as you
balance
yourself

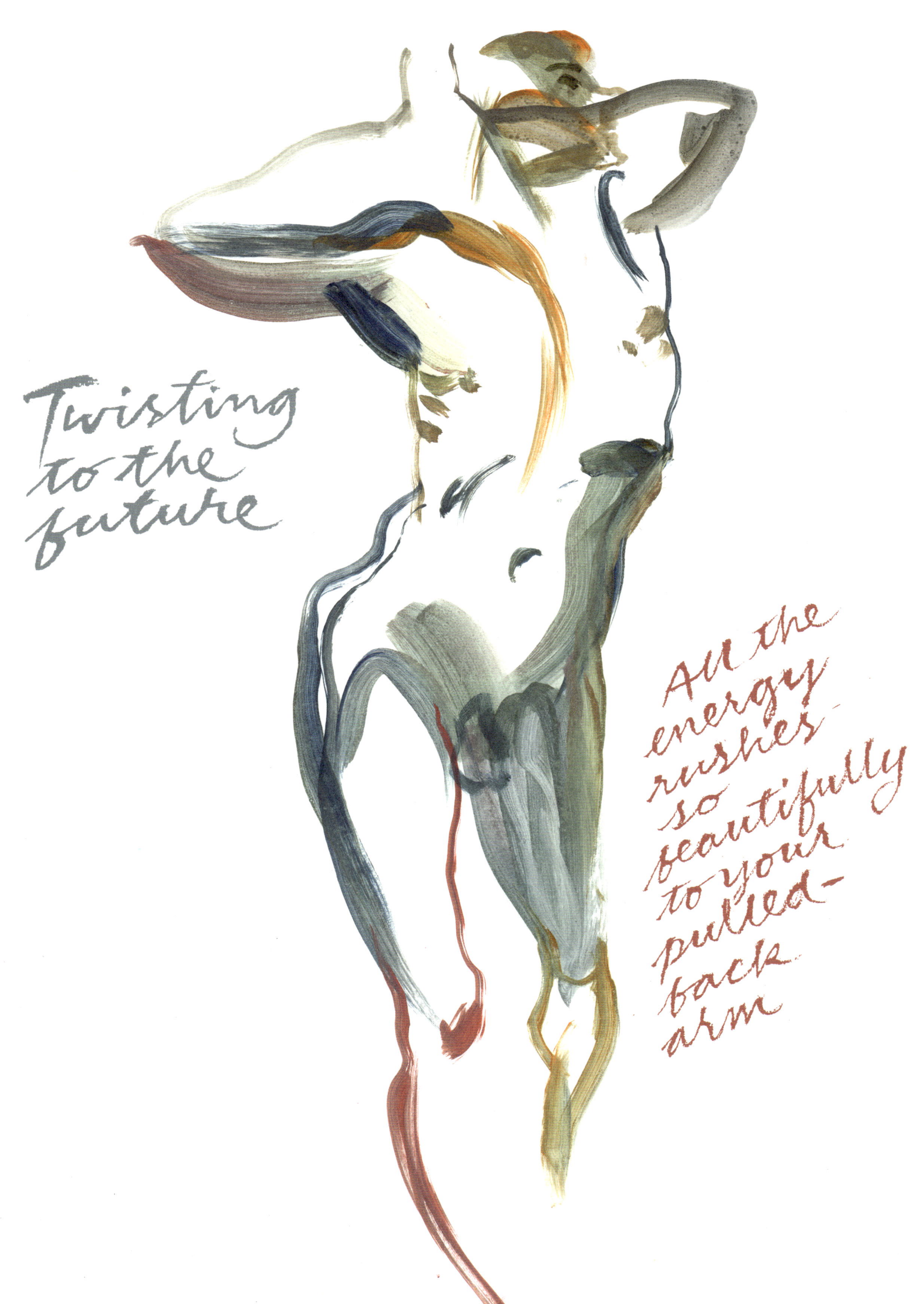

Twisting
to the
future

All the
energy
rushes
so
beautifully
to your
pulled-
back
arm

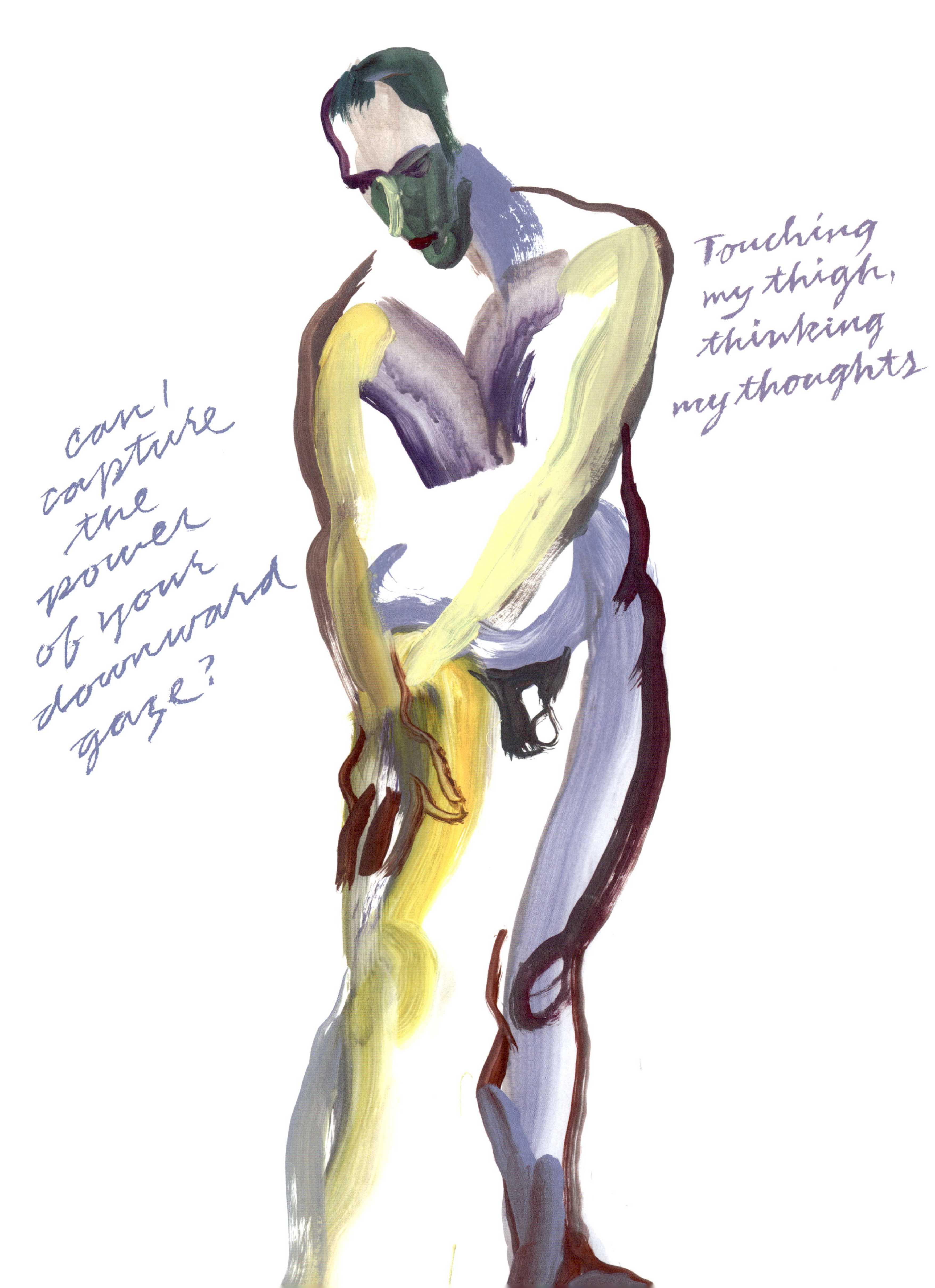
can I
capture
the
power
of your
downward
gaze?

Touching
my thigh,
thinking
my thoughts

a conversation with my hand
your voluptuous thigh moves your leg forward dramatically

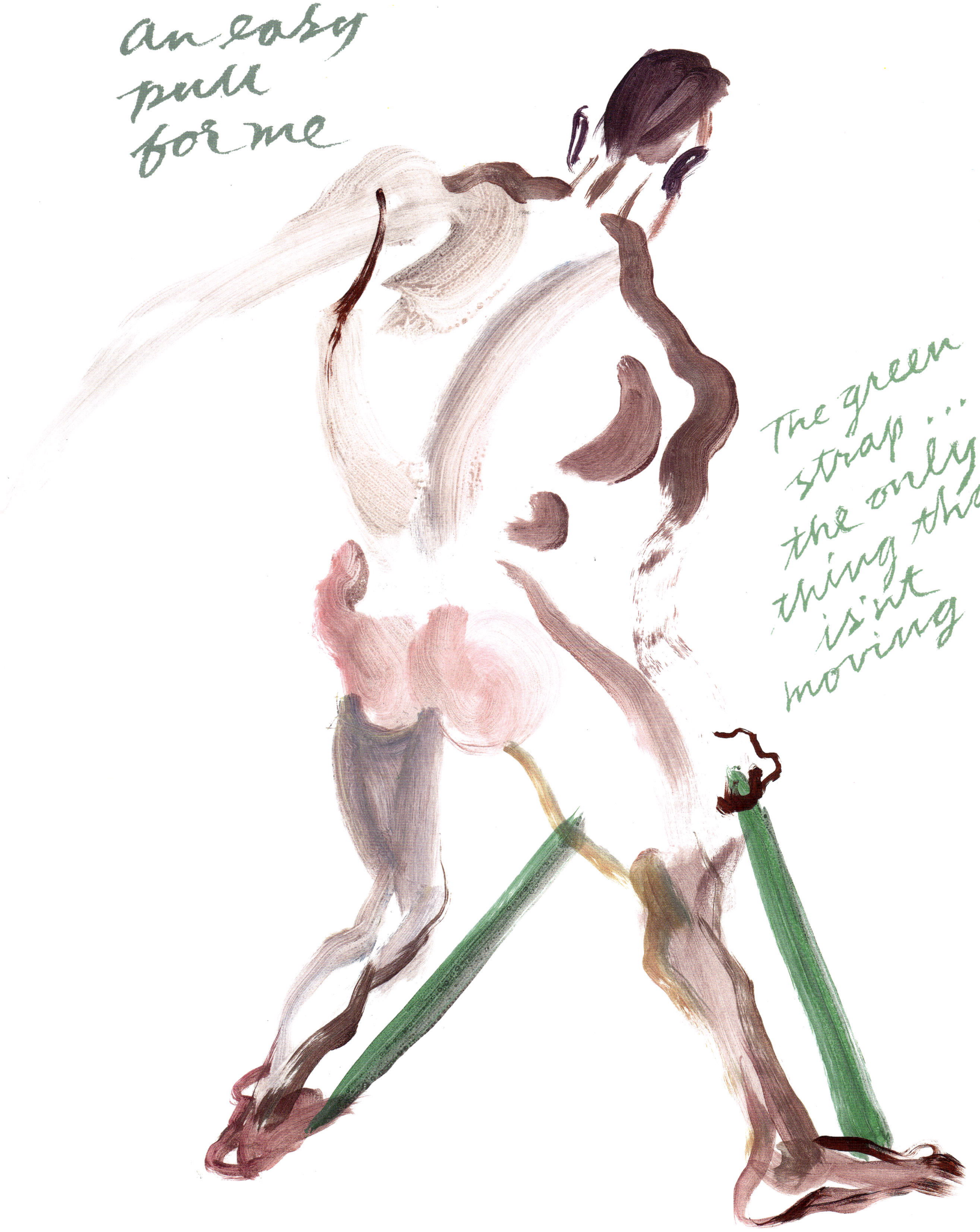

an easy
pull
for me

The green
strap ...
the only
thing that
is'nt
moving

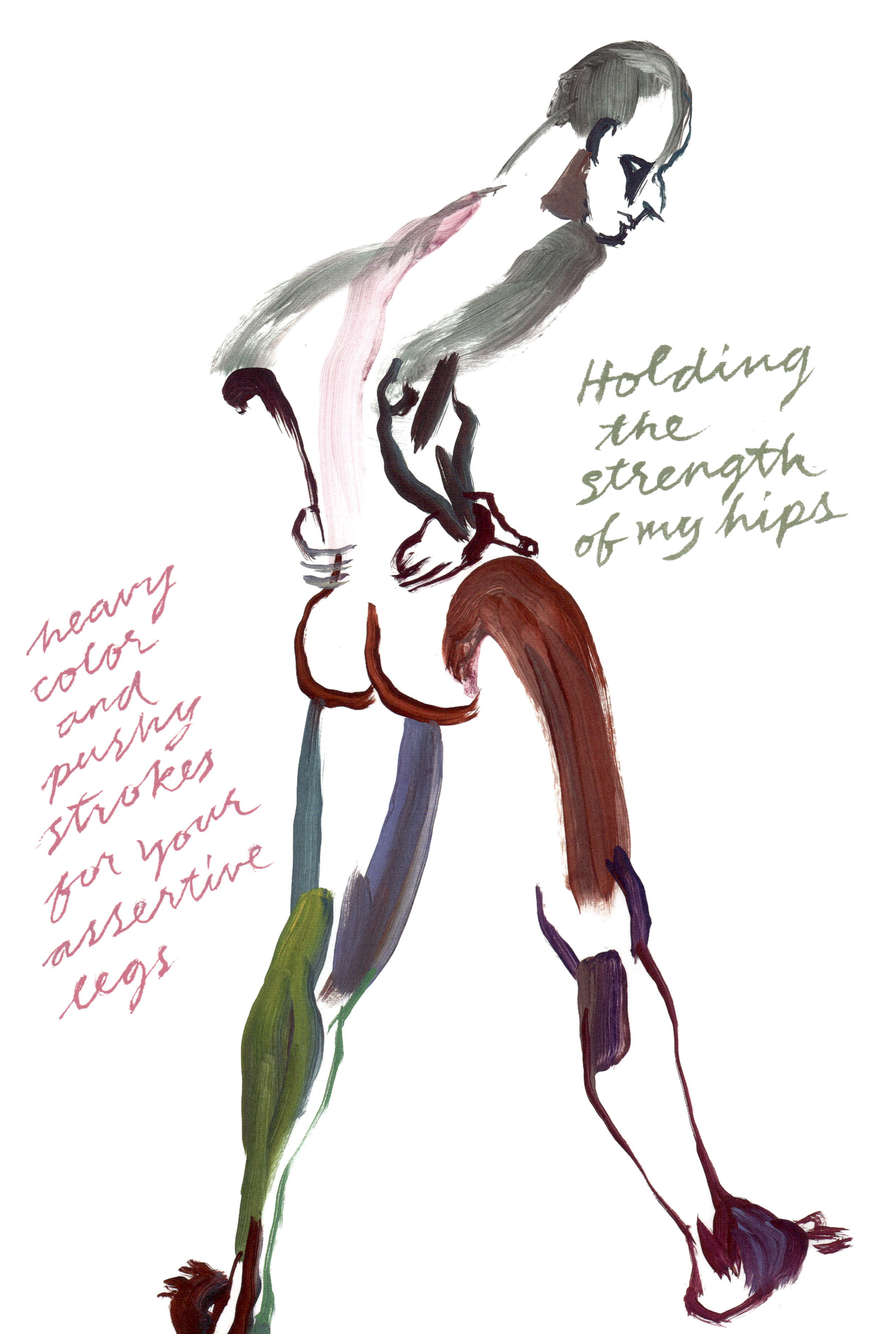

Holding
the
strength
of my hips

heavy
color
and
pushy
strokes
for your
assertive
legs

Hand,
the past,
penis,
the future

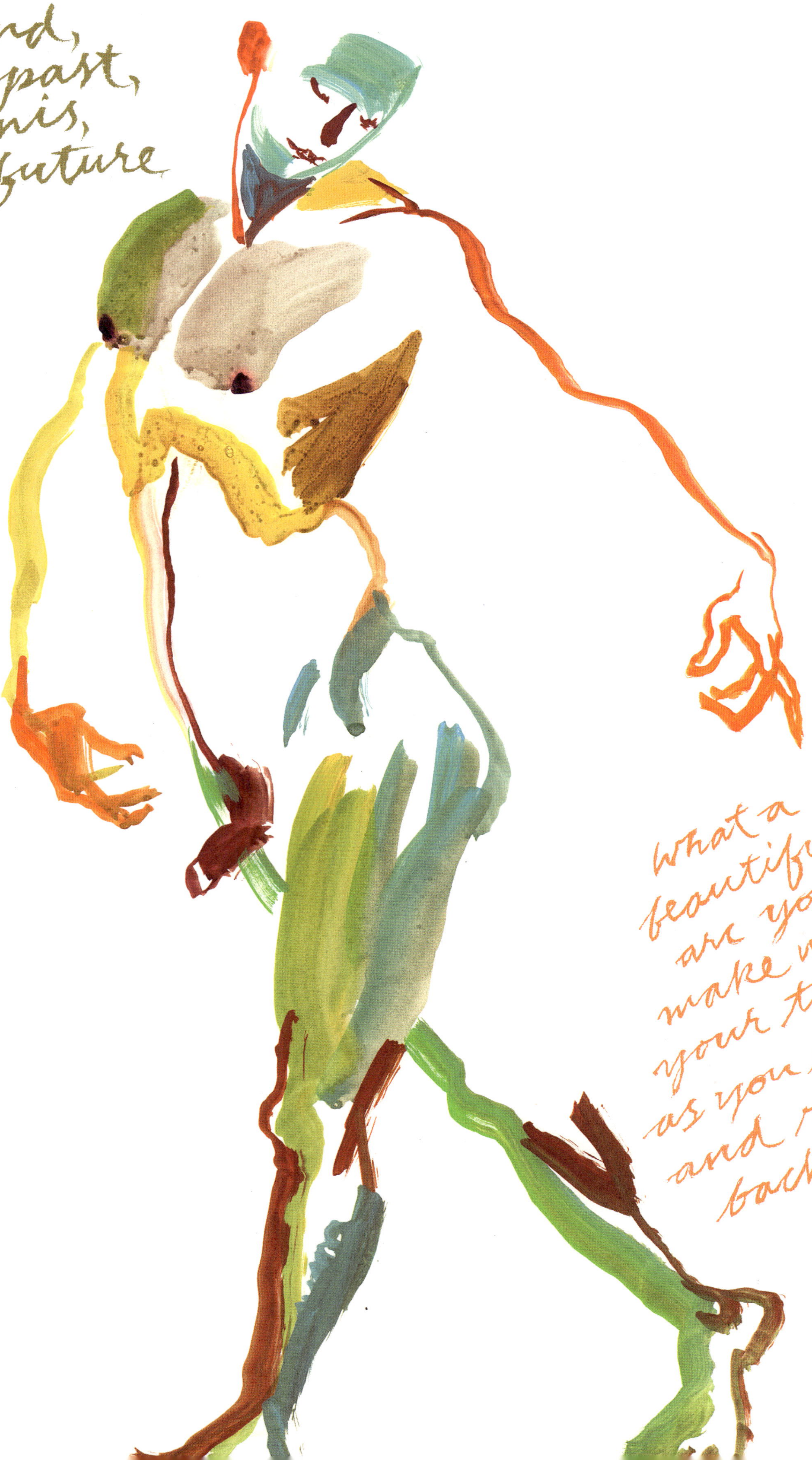

what a
beautiful
are you
make with
your torso
as you look
and reach
back

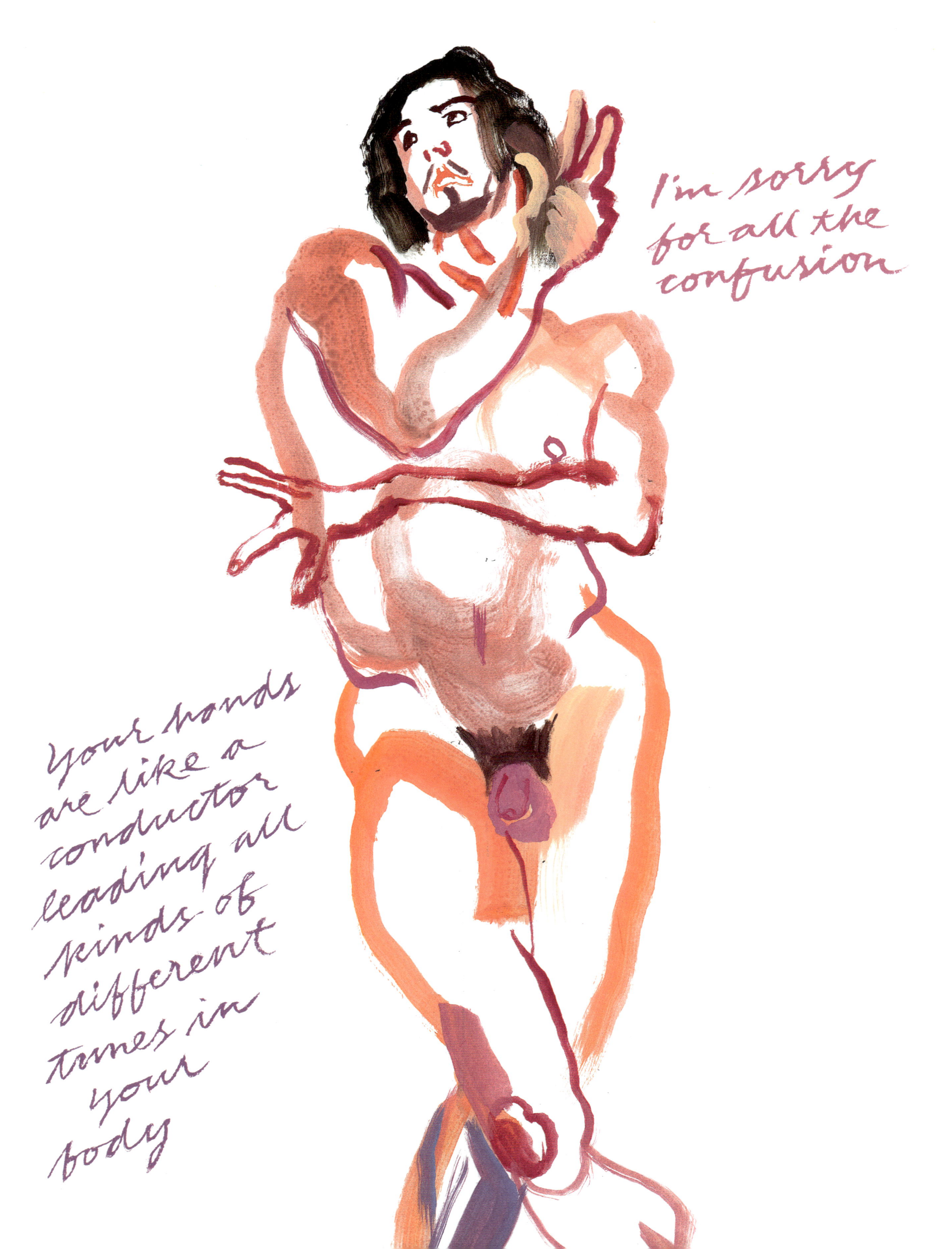
I'm sorry
for all the
confusion

Your hands
are like a
conductor
leading all
kinds of
different
tunes in
your
body

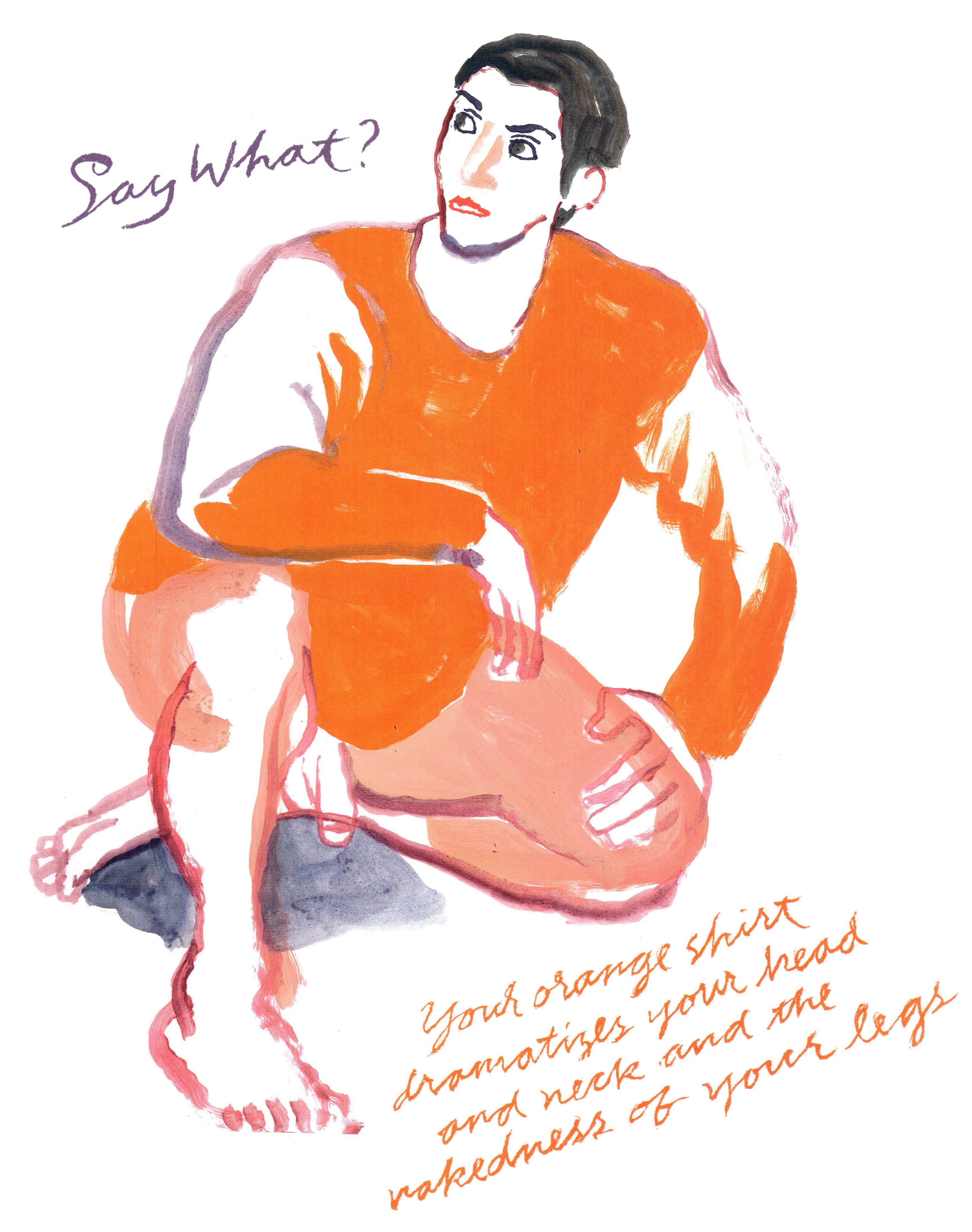

Say What?
Your orange shirt
dramatizes your head
and neck and the
nakedness of your legs

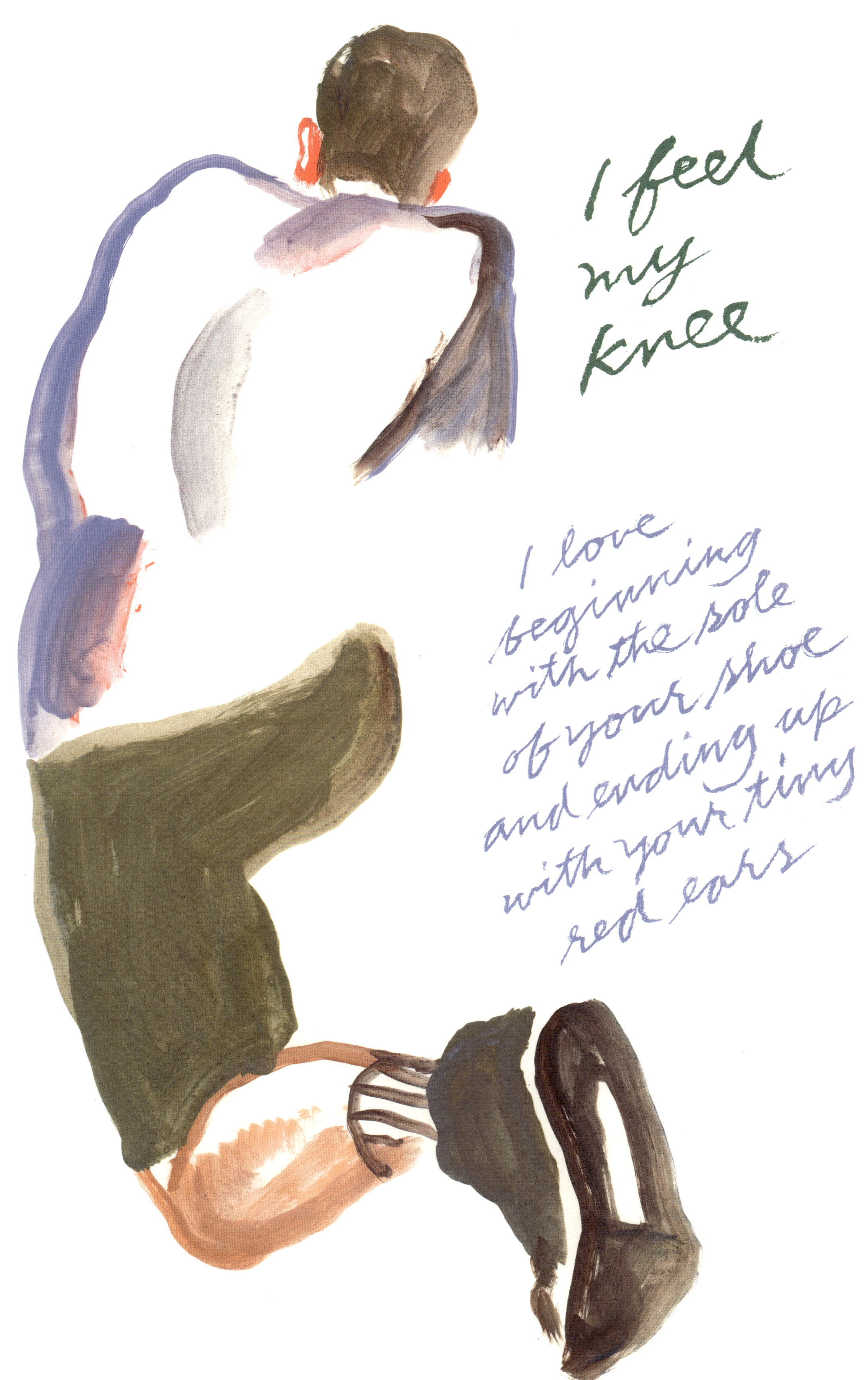

I feel
my
knee

I love
beginning
with the sole
of your shoe
and ending up
with your tiny
red ears

Something out there gets my goat
you are so round round round in your body but so spiky in your face

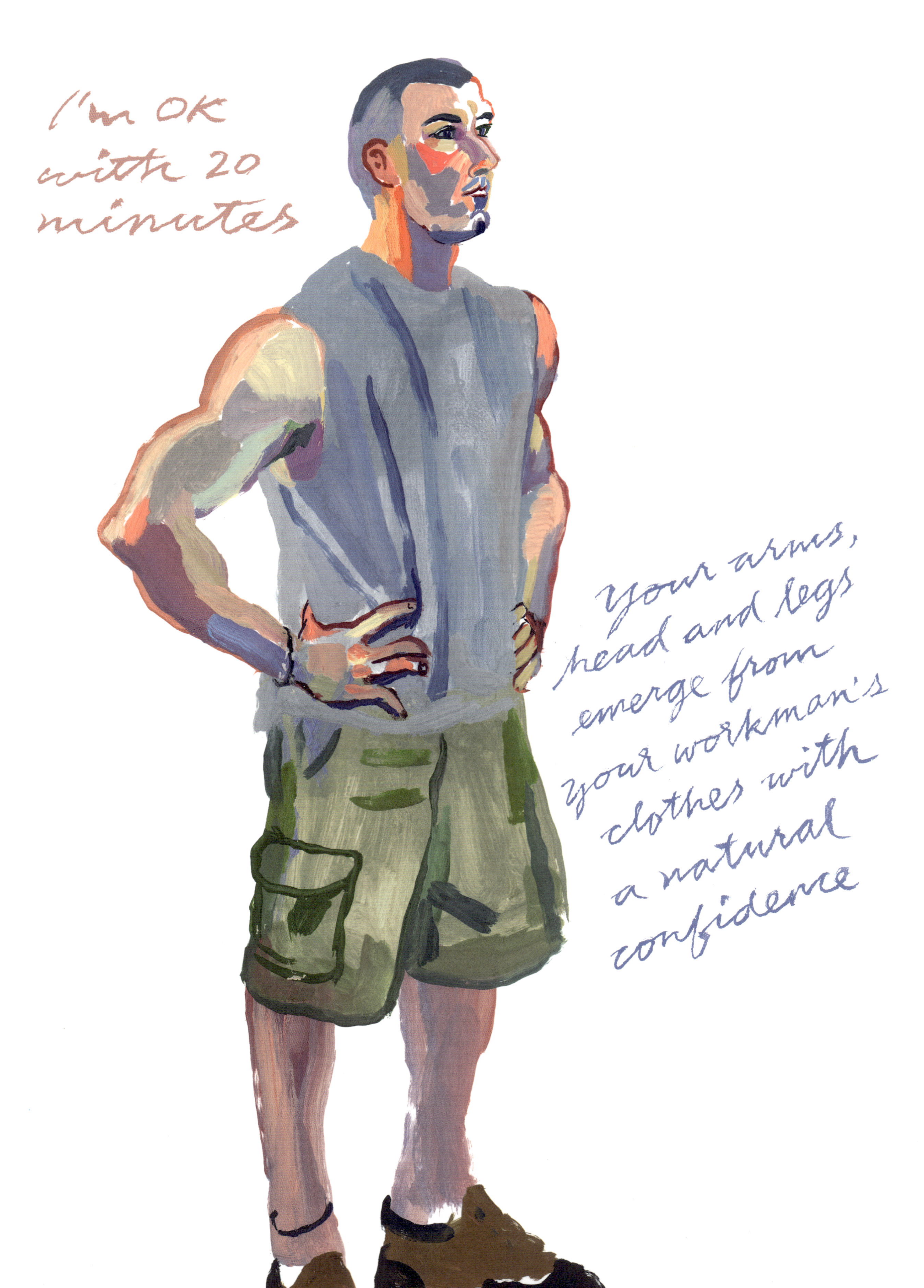

I'm OK with 20 minutes
Your arms, head and legs emerge from your workman's clothes with a natural confidence

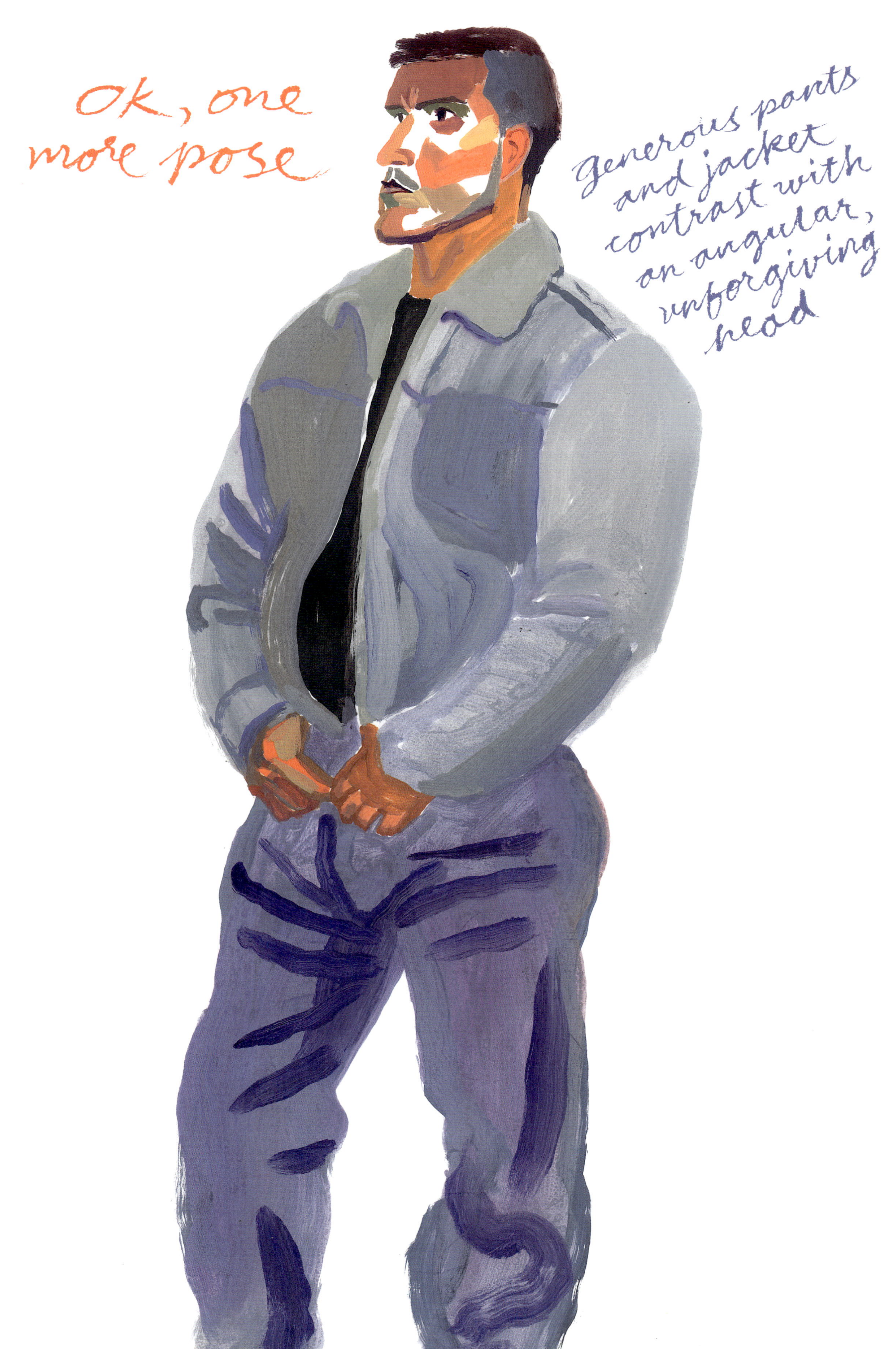
ok, one
more pose
generous pants
and jacket
contrast with
an angular,
unforgiving
head

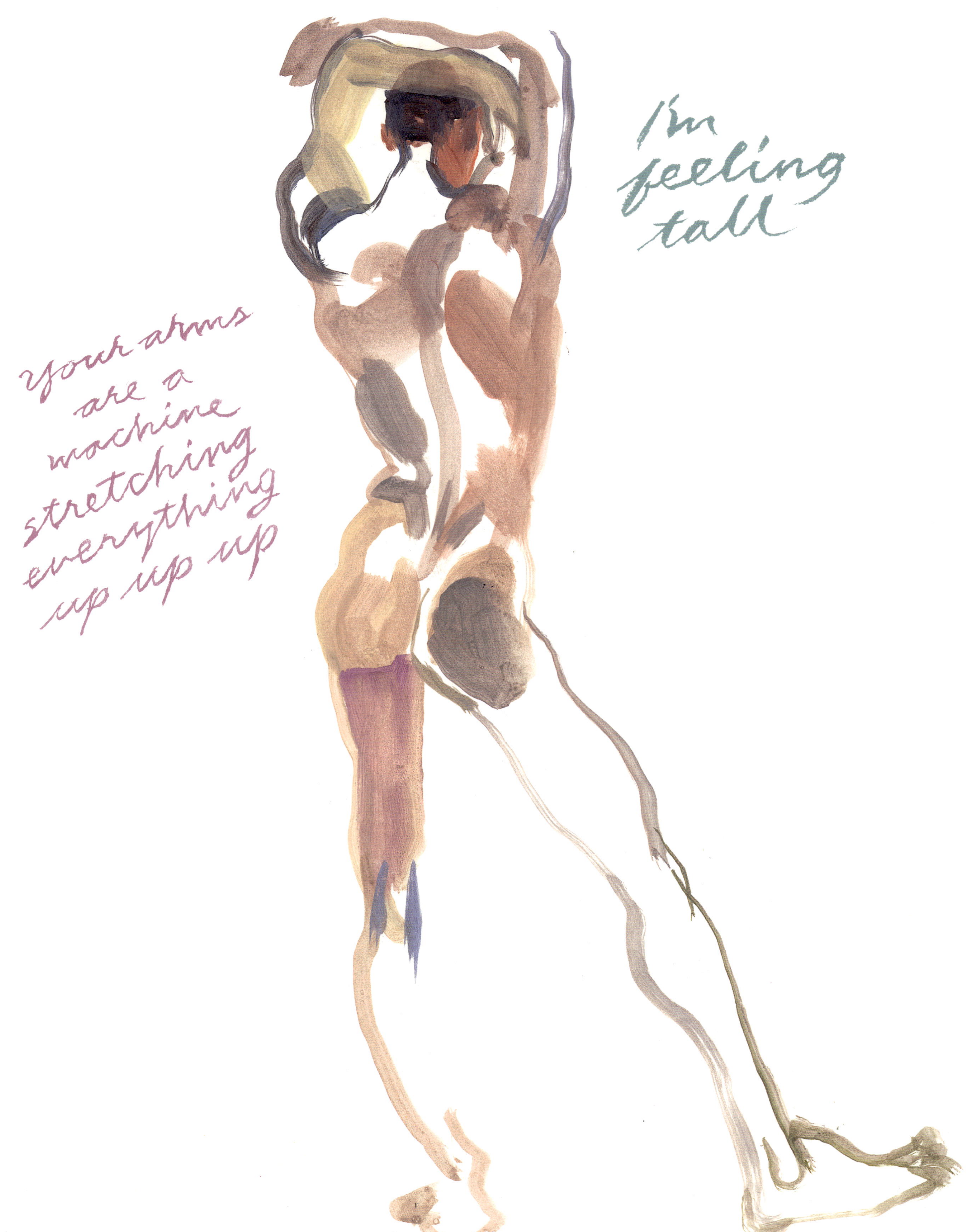

I'm
feeling
tall

your arms
are a
machine
stretching
everything
up up up

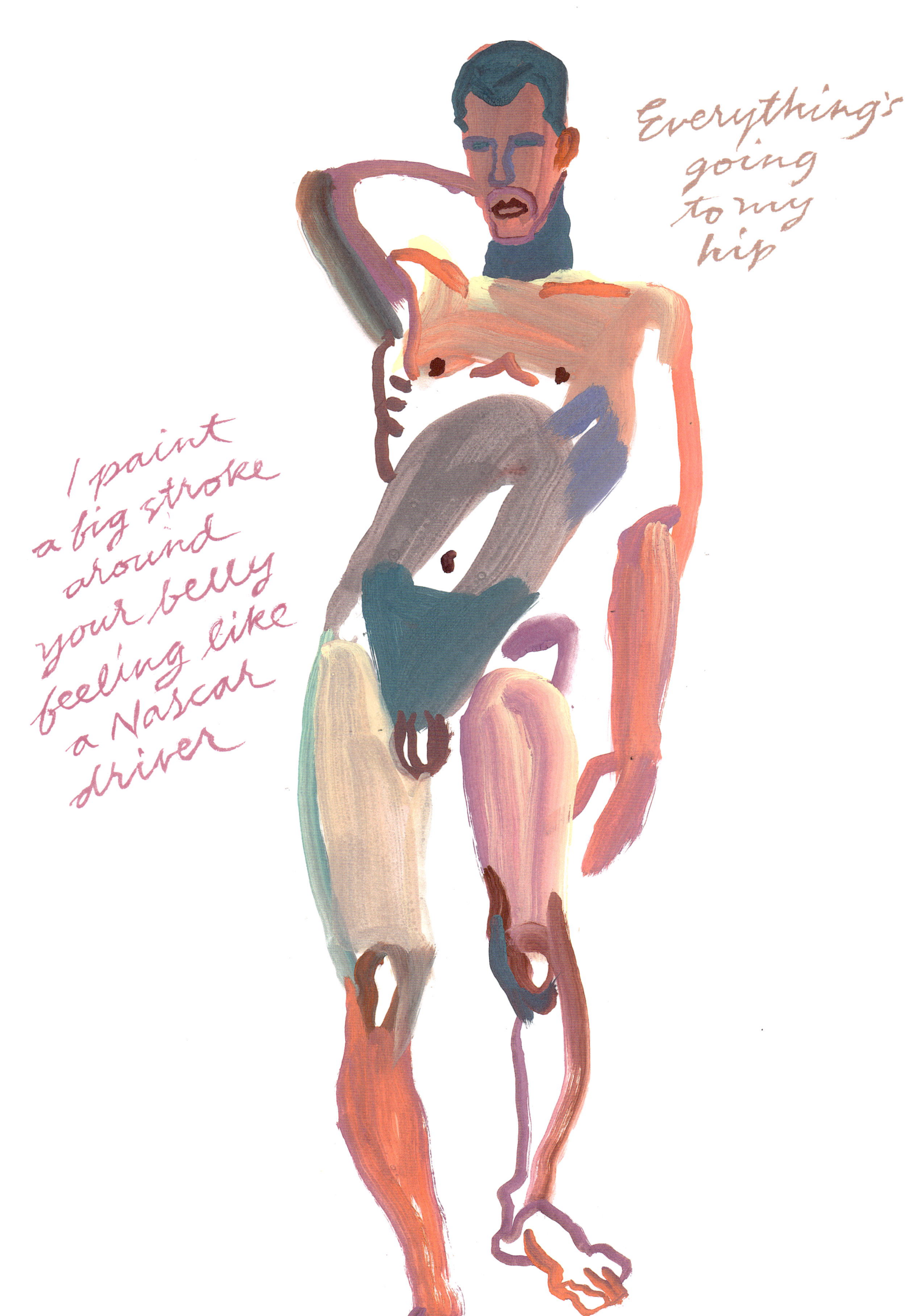
Everything's
going
to my
hip

I paint
a big stroke
around
your belly
feeling like
a Nascar
driver

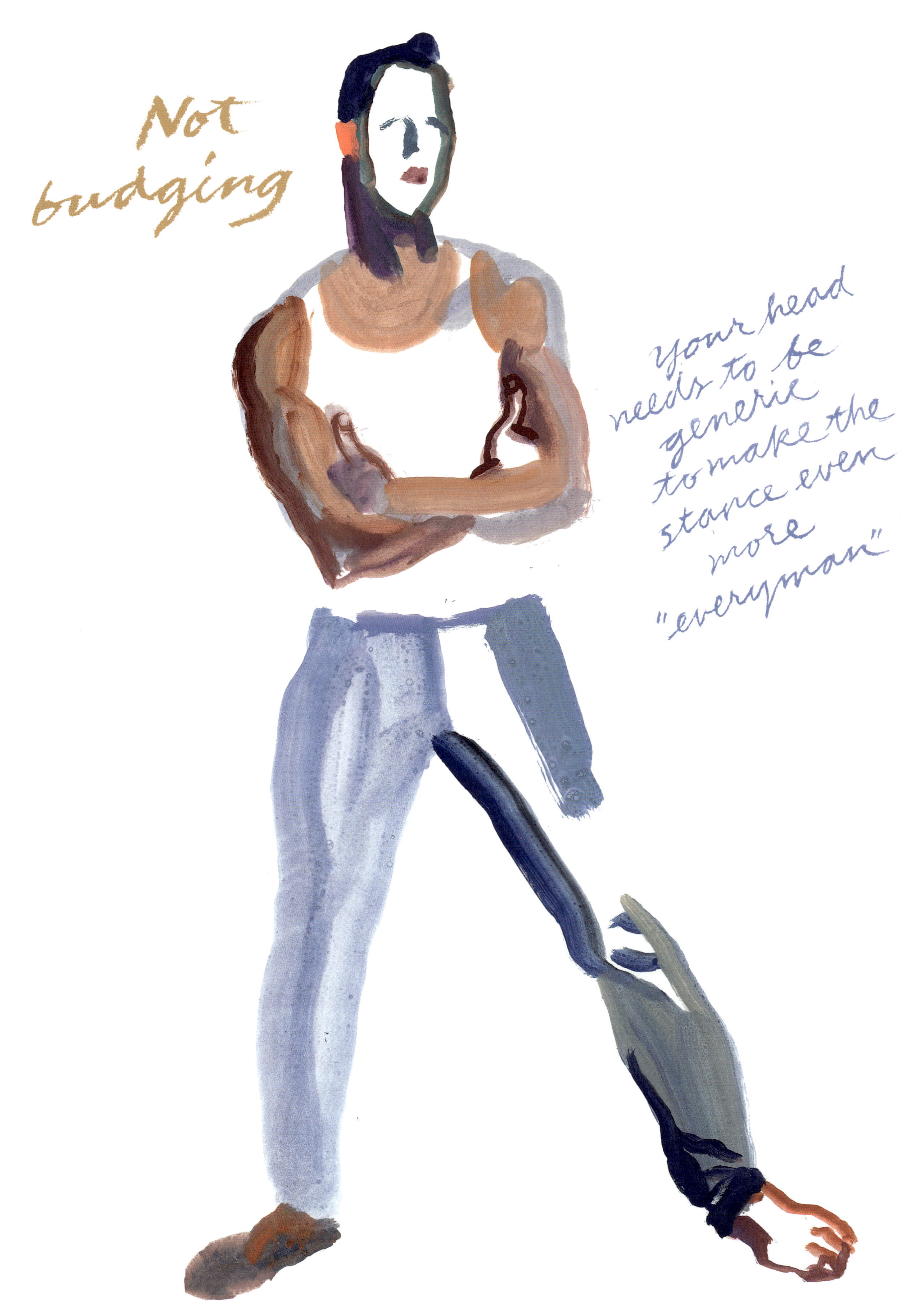
Not
budging

your head
needs to be
generic
to make the
stance even
more
"everyman"

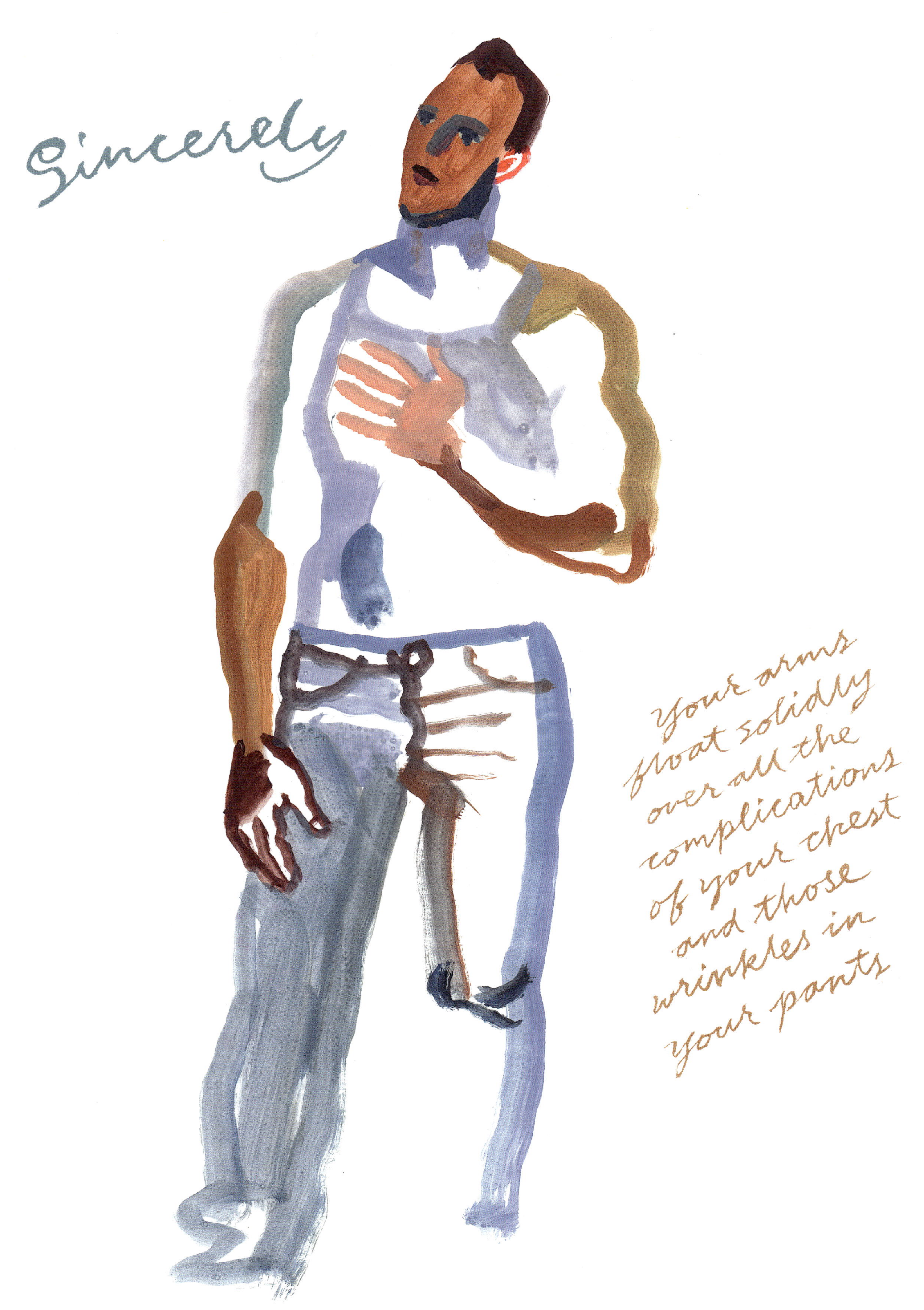

Sincerely

Your arms
float solidly
over all the
complications
of your chest
and those
wrinkles in
your pants

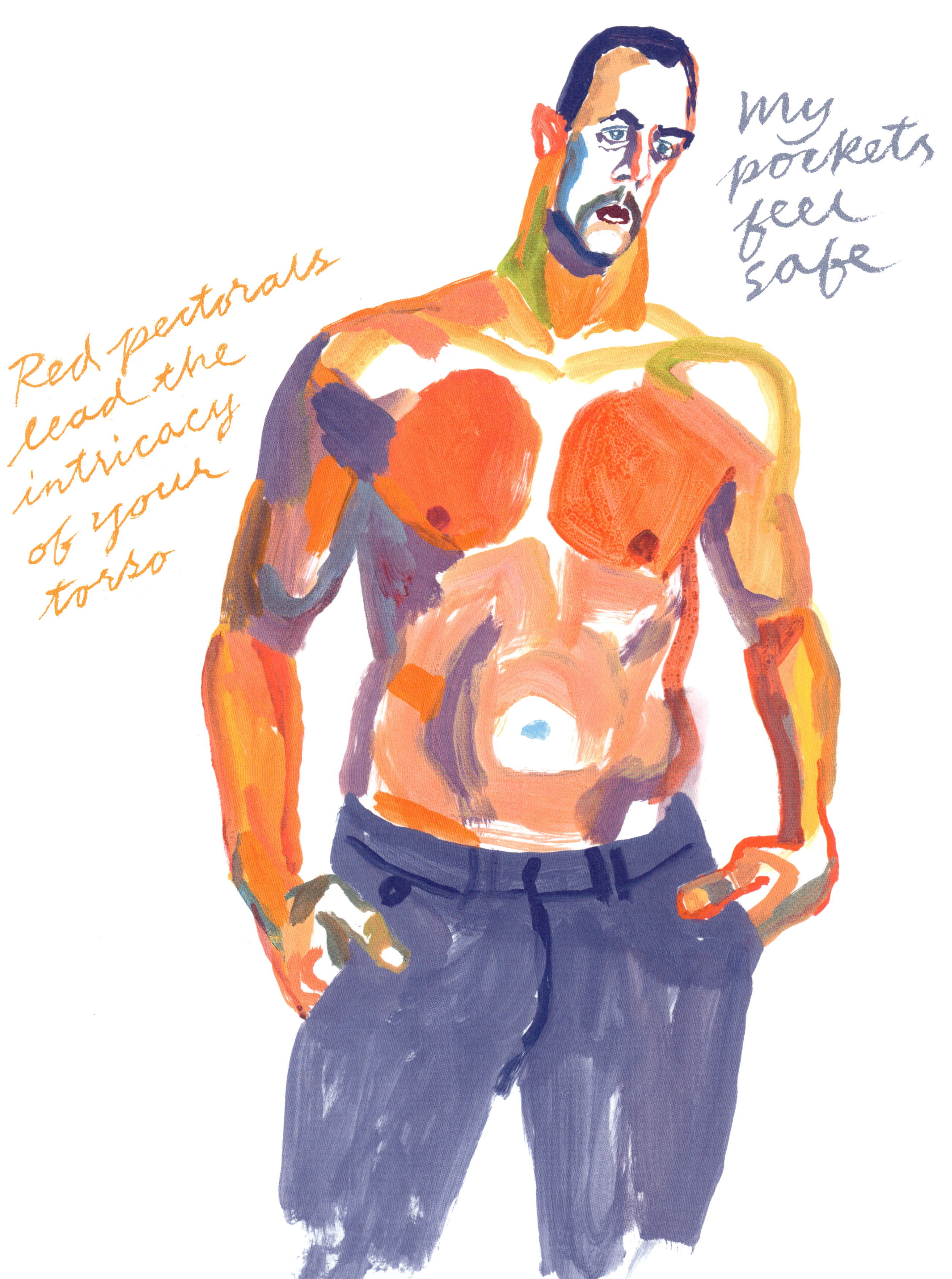
Red pectorals
lead the
intricacy
of your
torso
my
pockets
feel
safe

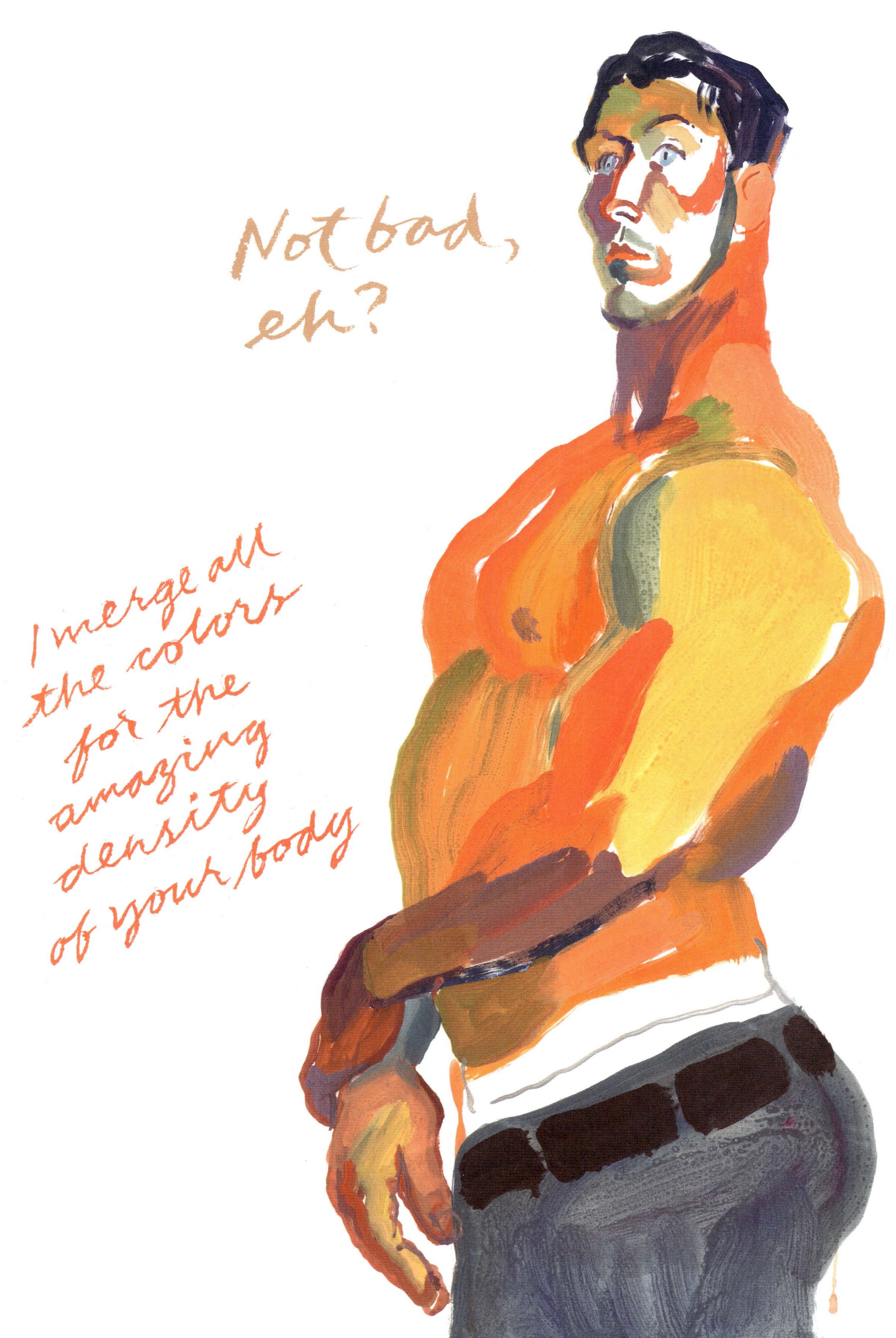

Not bad, eh?
I merge all the colors for the amazing density of your body

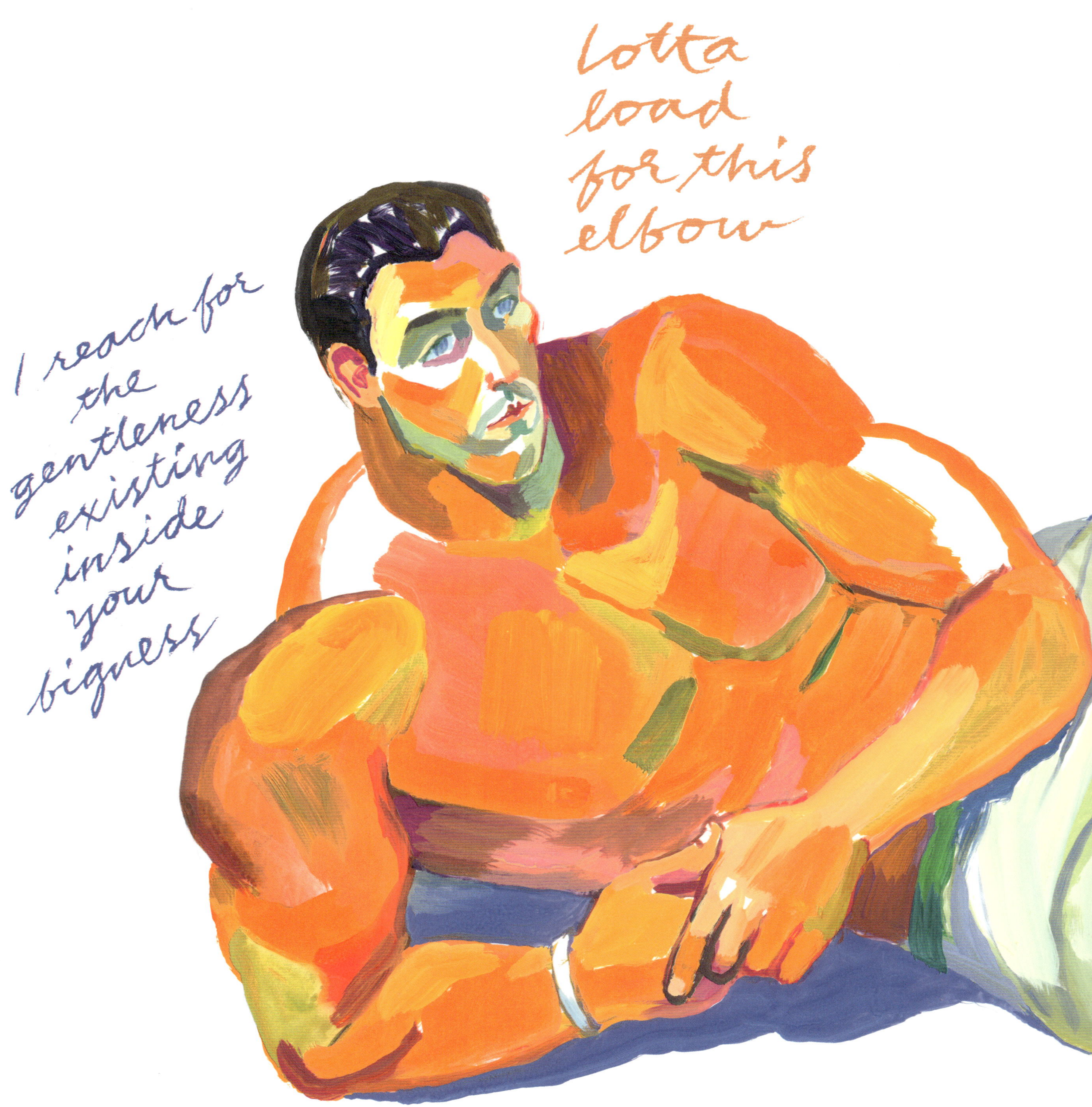
lotta
load
for this
elbow

I reach for
the
gentleness
existing
inside
your
bigness

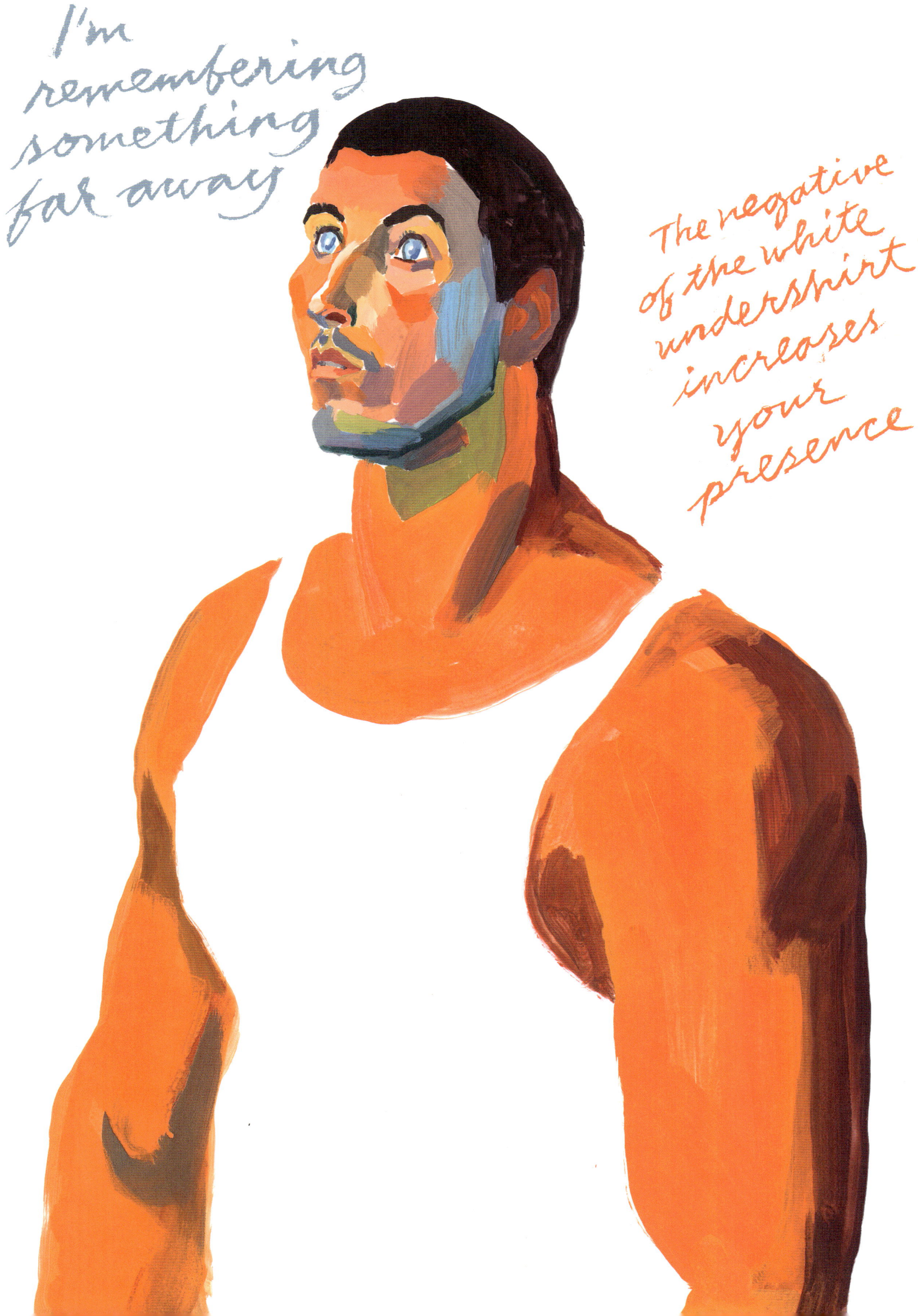

I'm
remembering
something
far away
The negative
of the white
undershirt
increases
your
presence

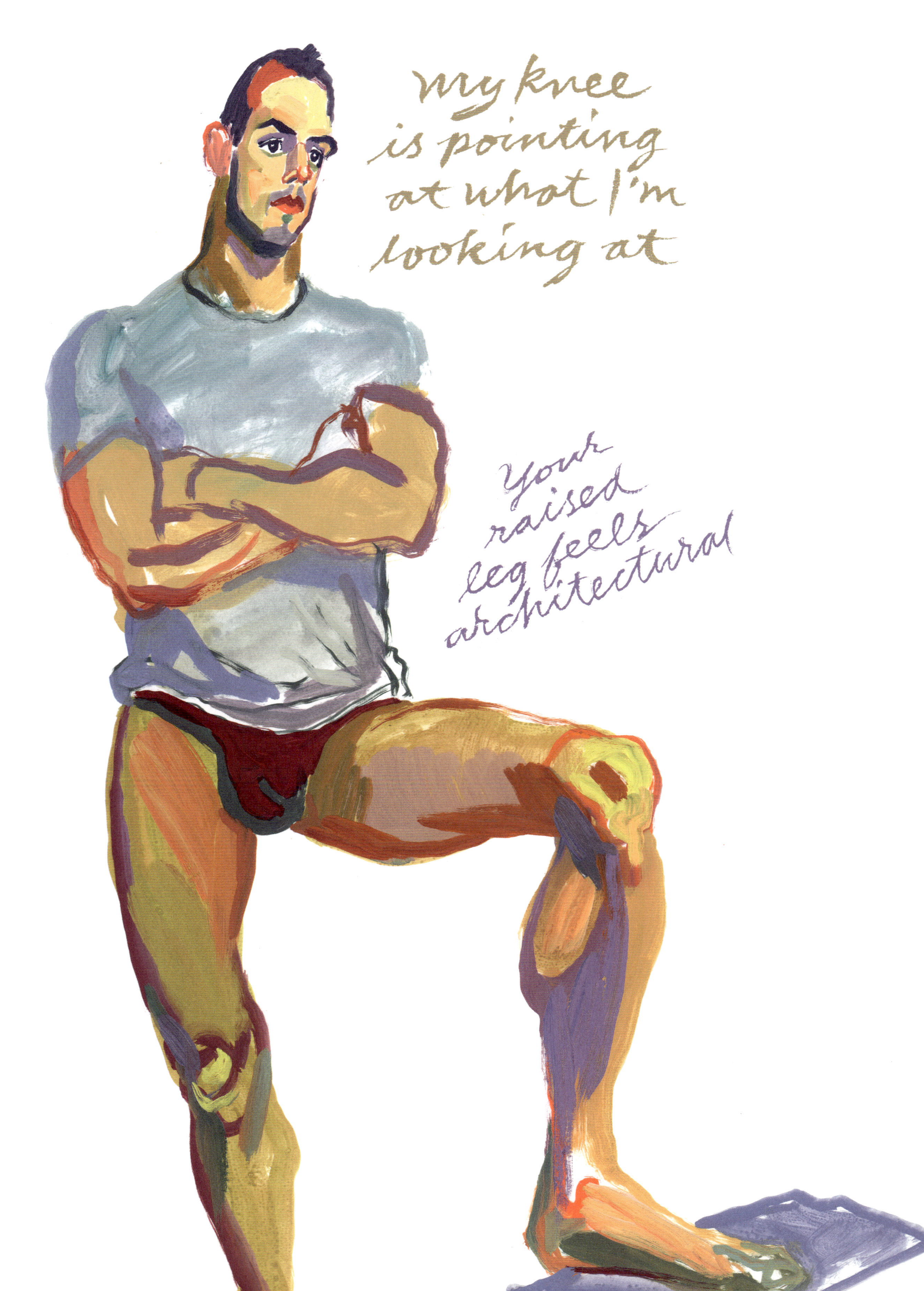

my knee
is pointing
at what I'm
looking at

your
raised
leg feels
architectural

Determination

I paint
the heavy
interlocking
arms echoing
the dark
complexity
of your
brow

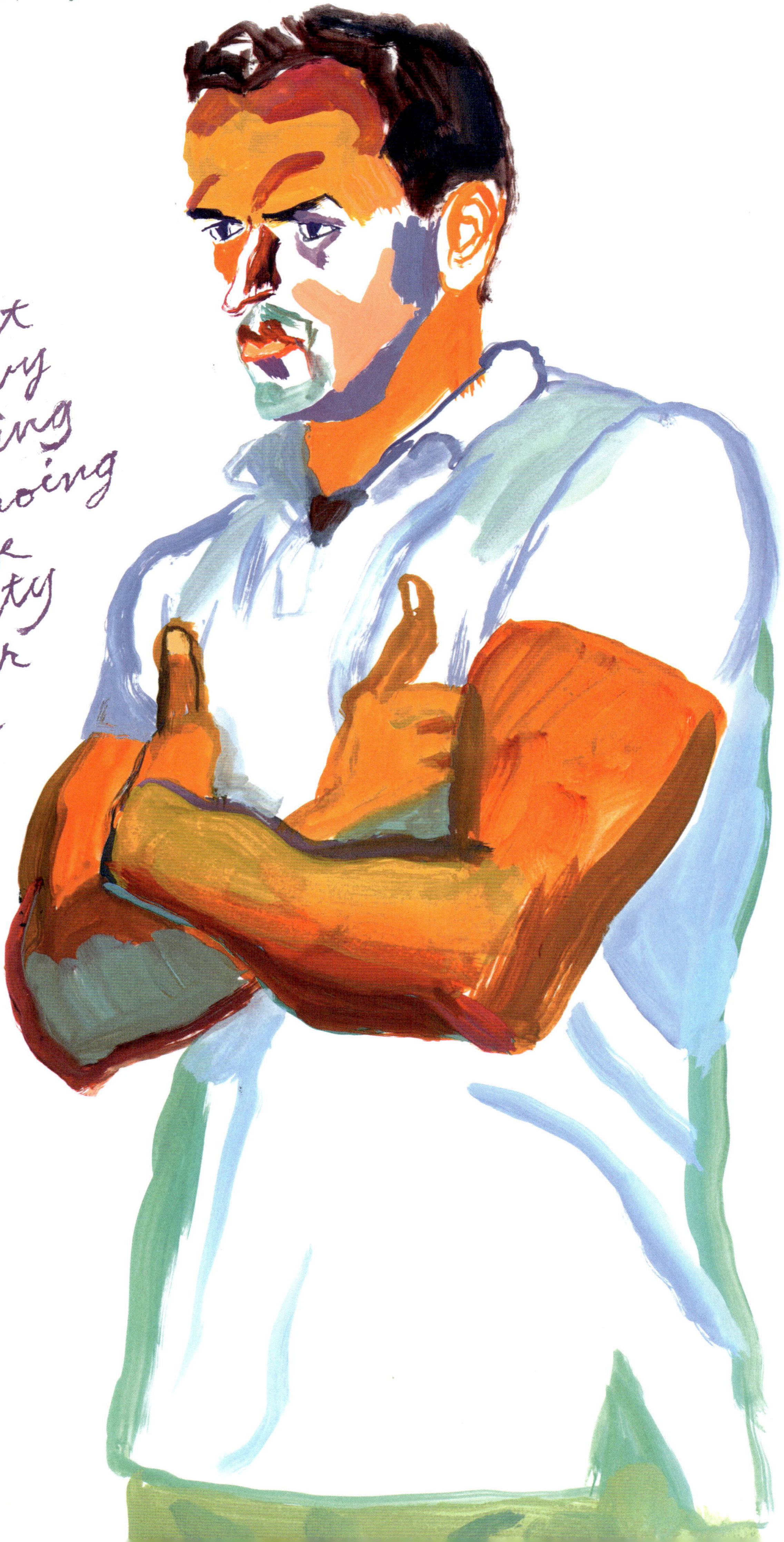

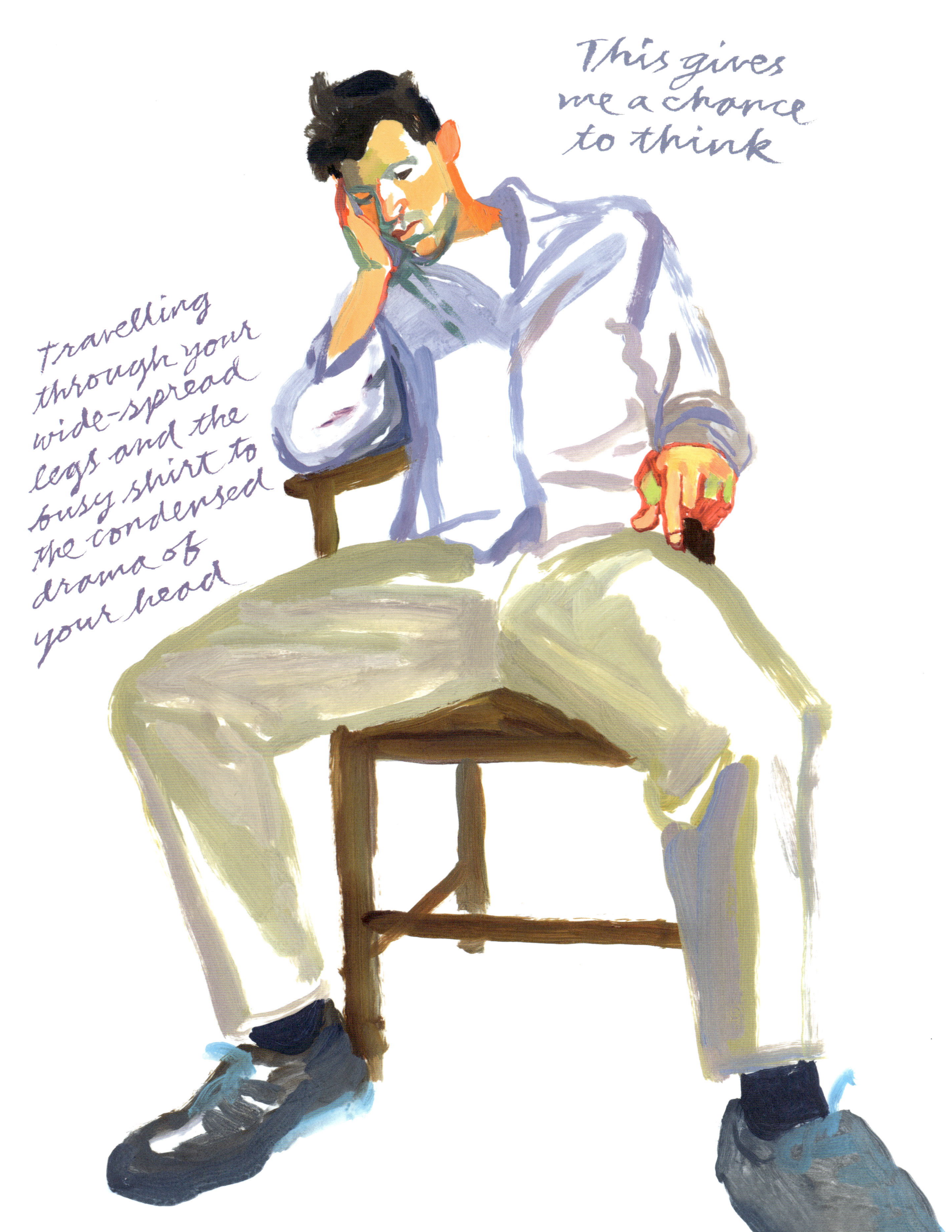
This gives me a chance to think

travelling through your wide-spread legs and the busy shirt to the condensed drama of your head

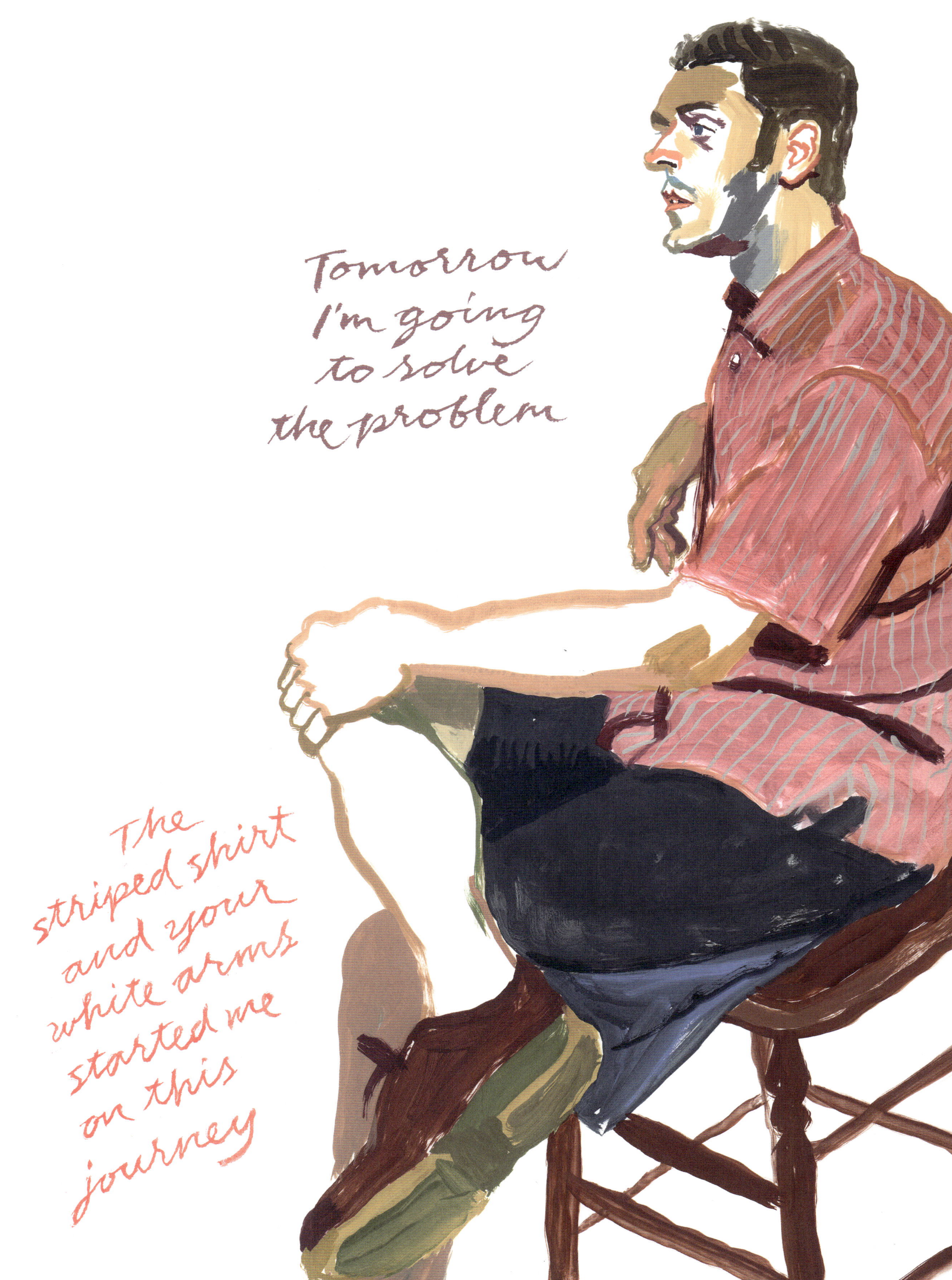
Tomorrow
I'm going
to solve
the problem

The
striped shirt
and your
white arms
started me
on this
journey

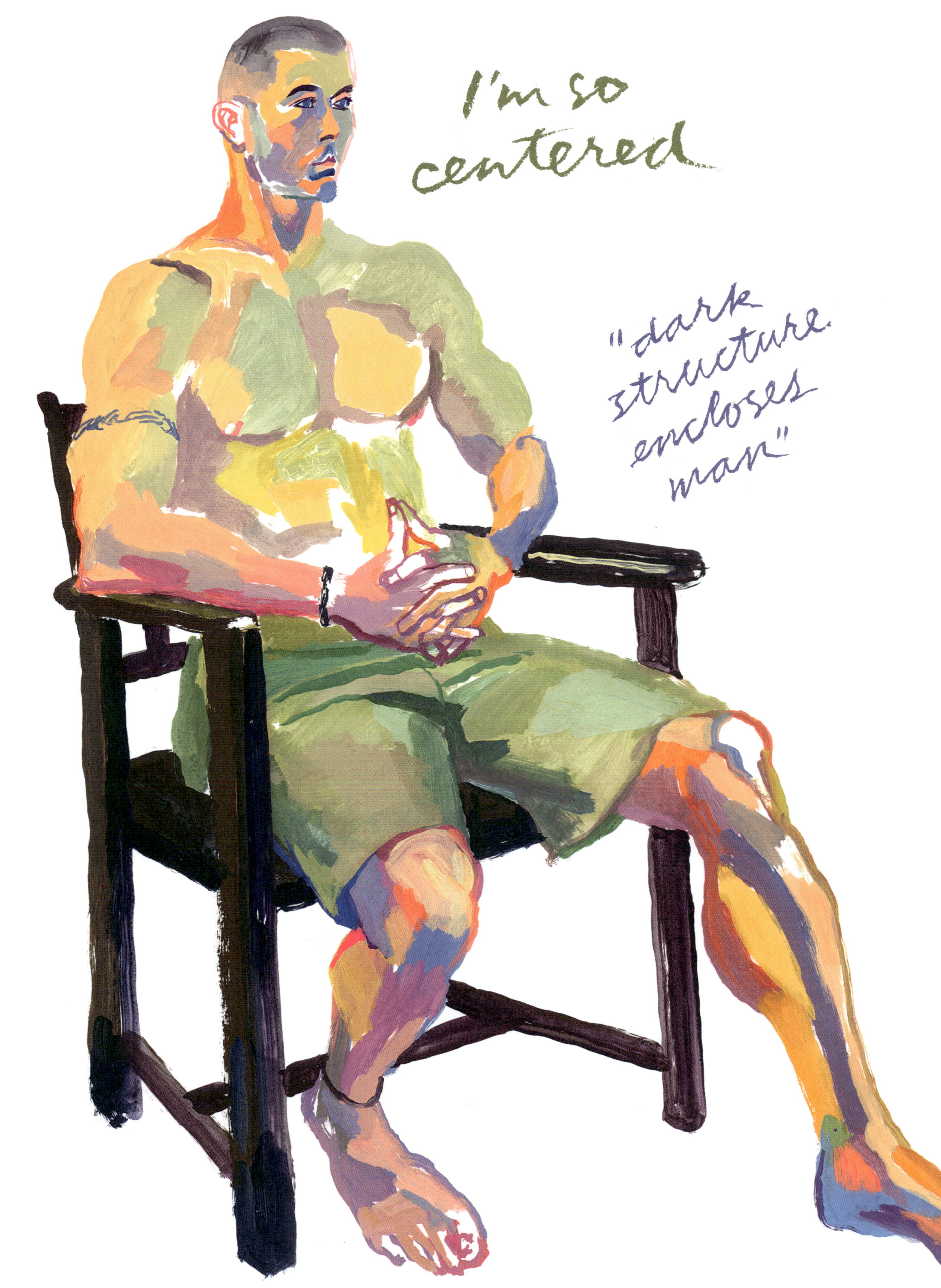

I'm so
centered
"dark
structure
encloses
man"

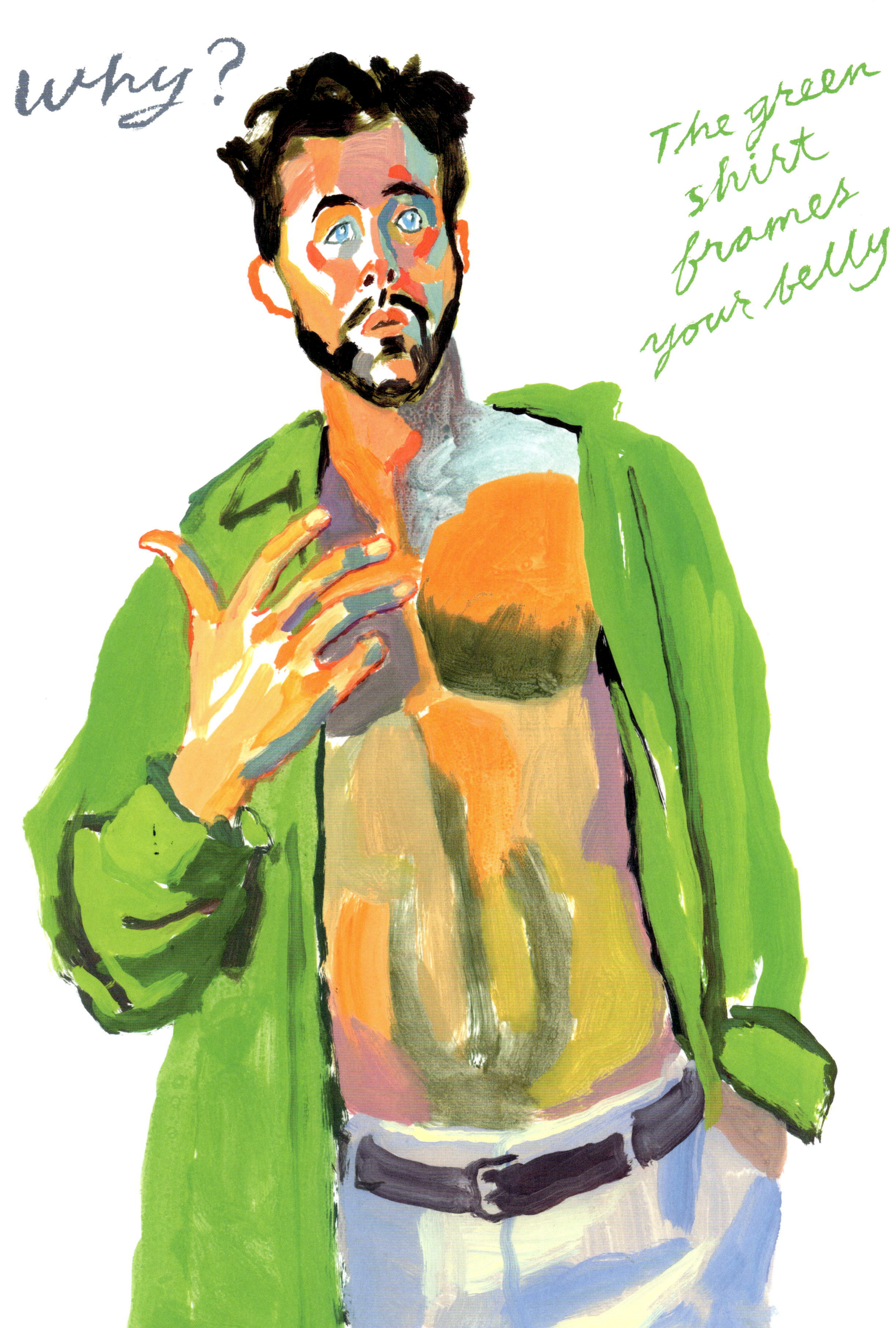

why?
The green shirt frames your belly

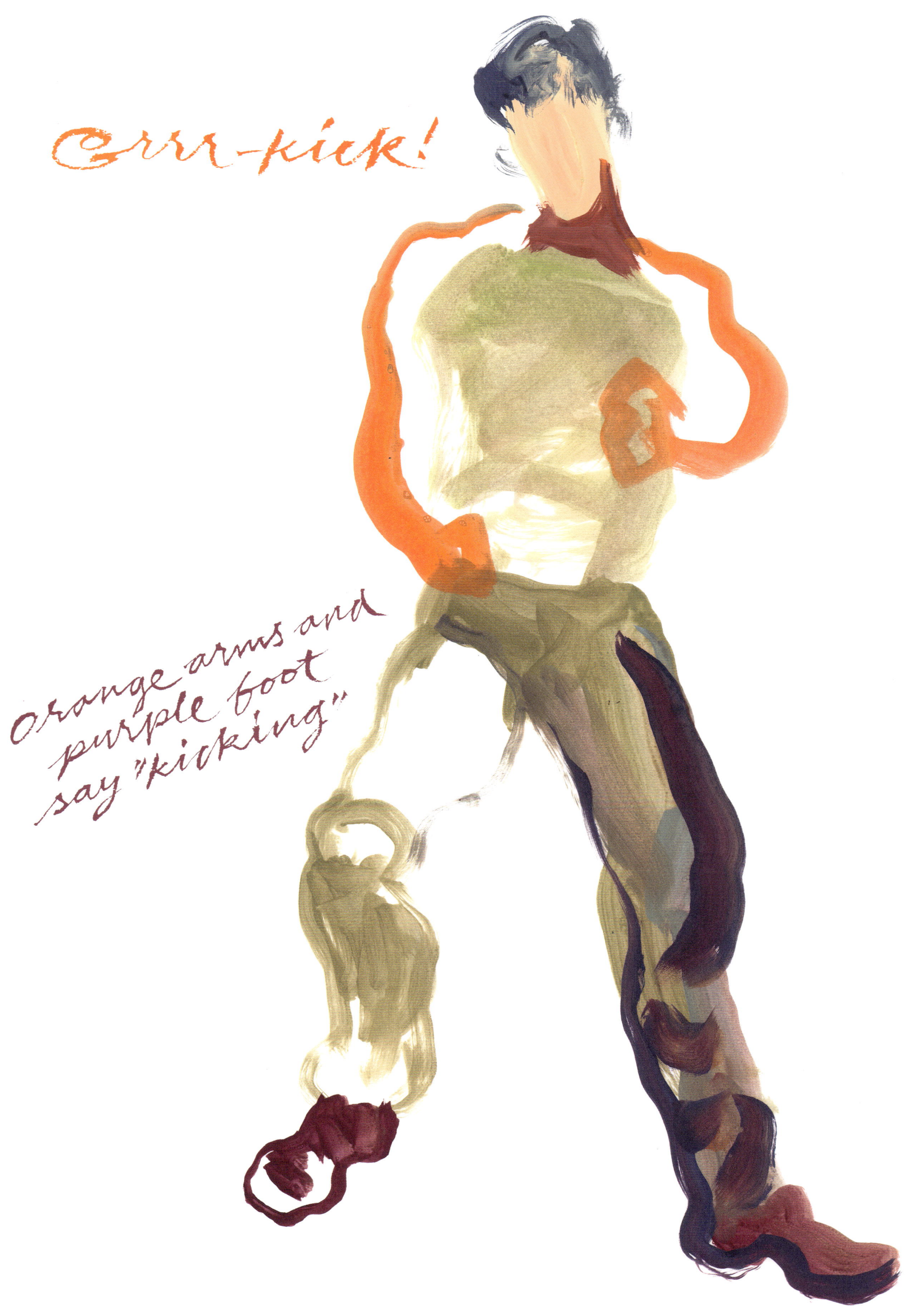

Grrr-kick!

orange arms and
purple foot
say "kicking"

I'm thoughtful
but not sad

The elegance
of your body
needs lines
moving
through air

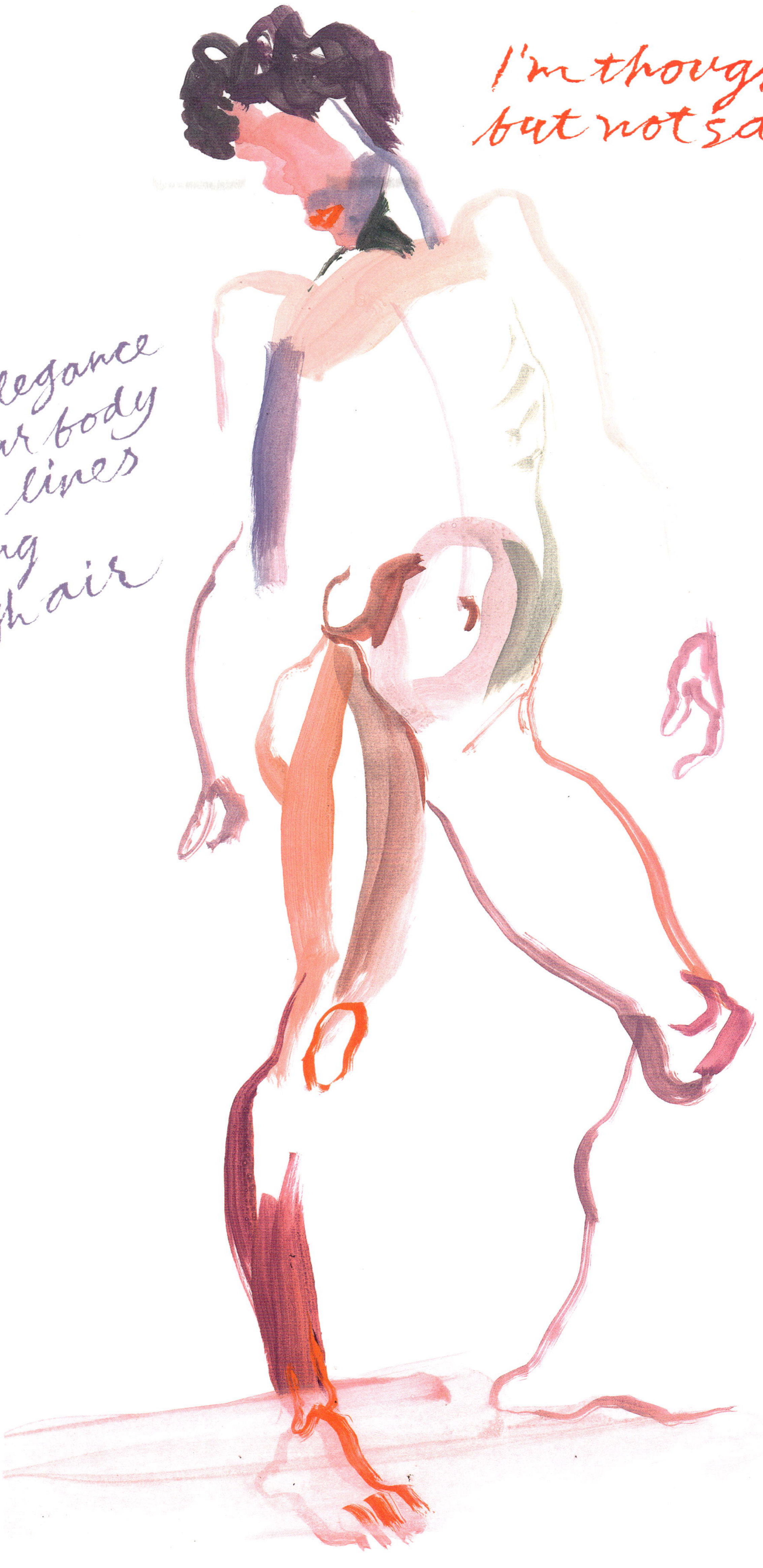

Reaching, Reaching

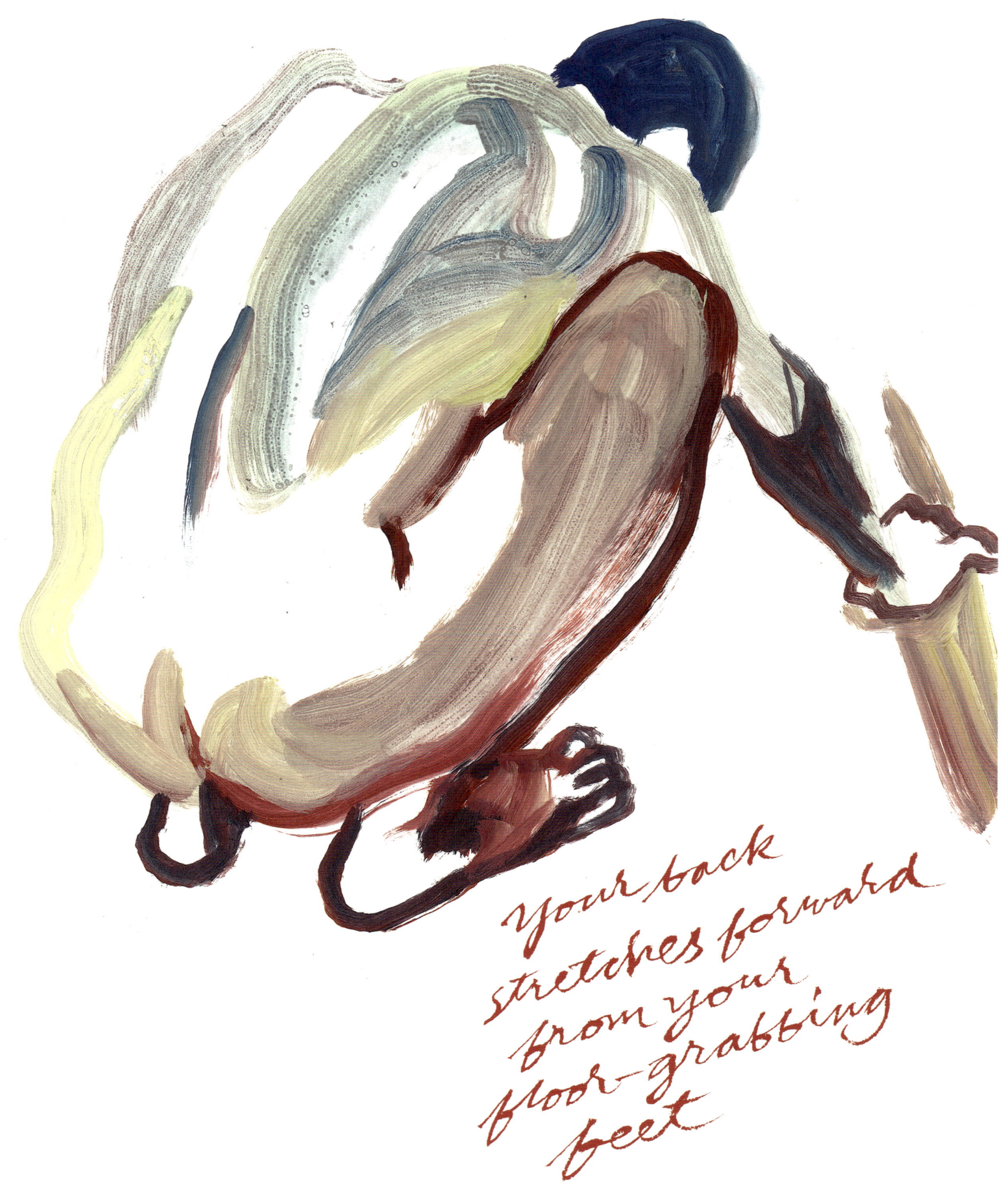

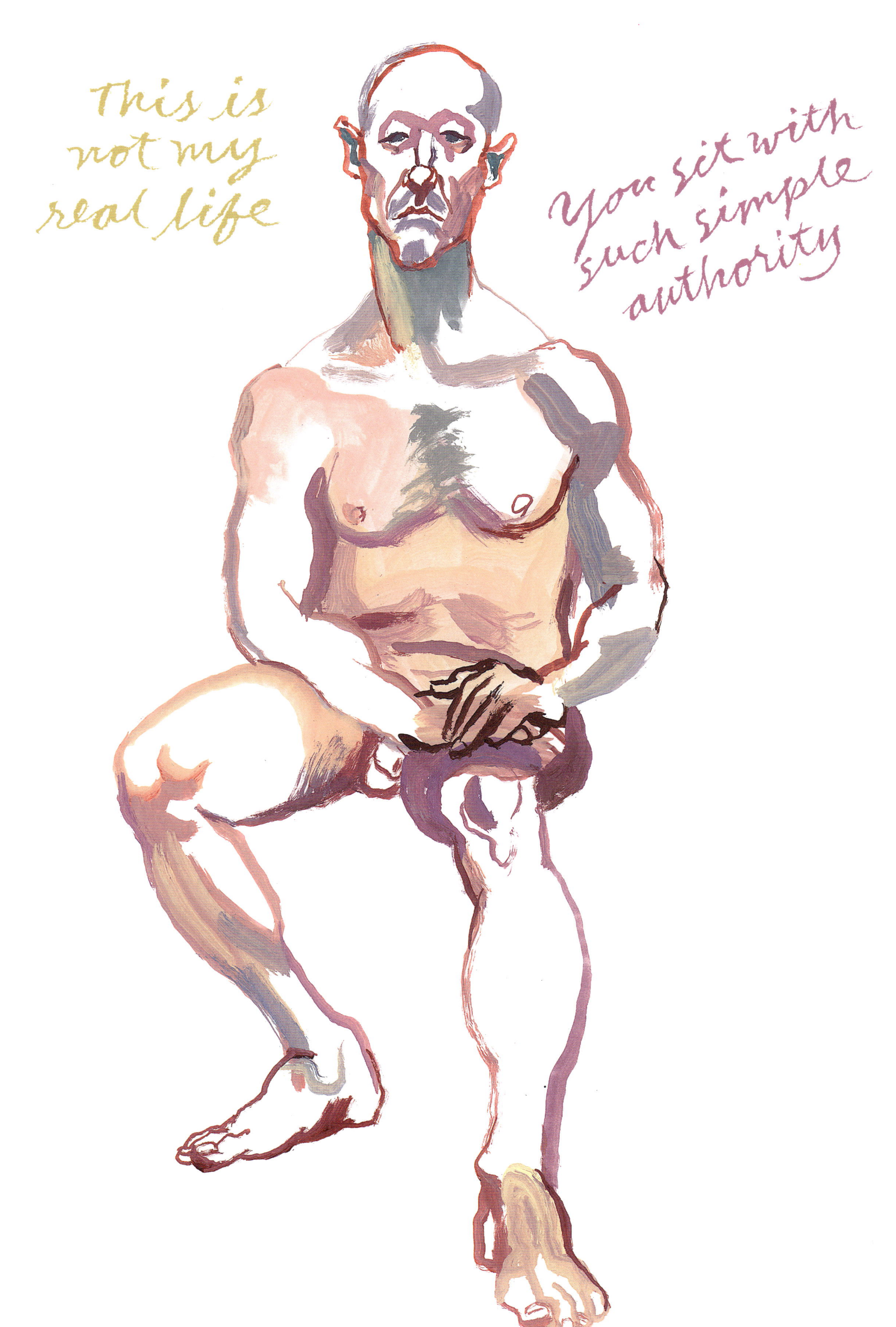
This is
not my
real life
You sit with
such simple
authority

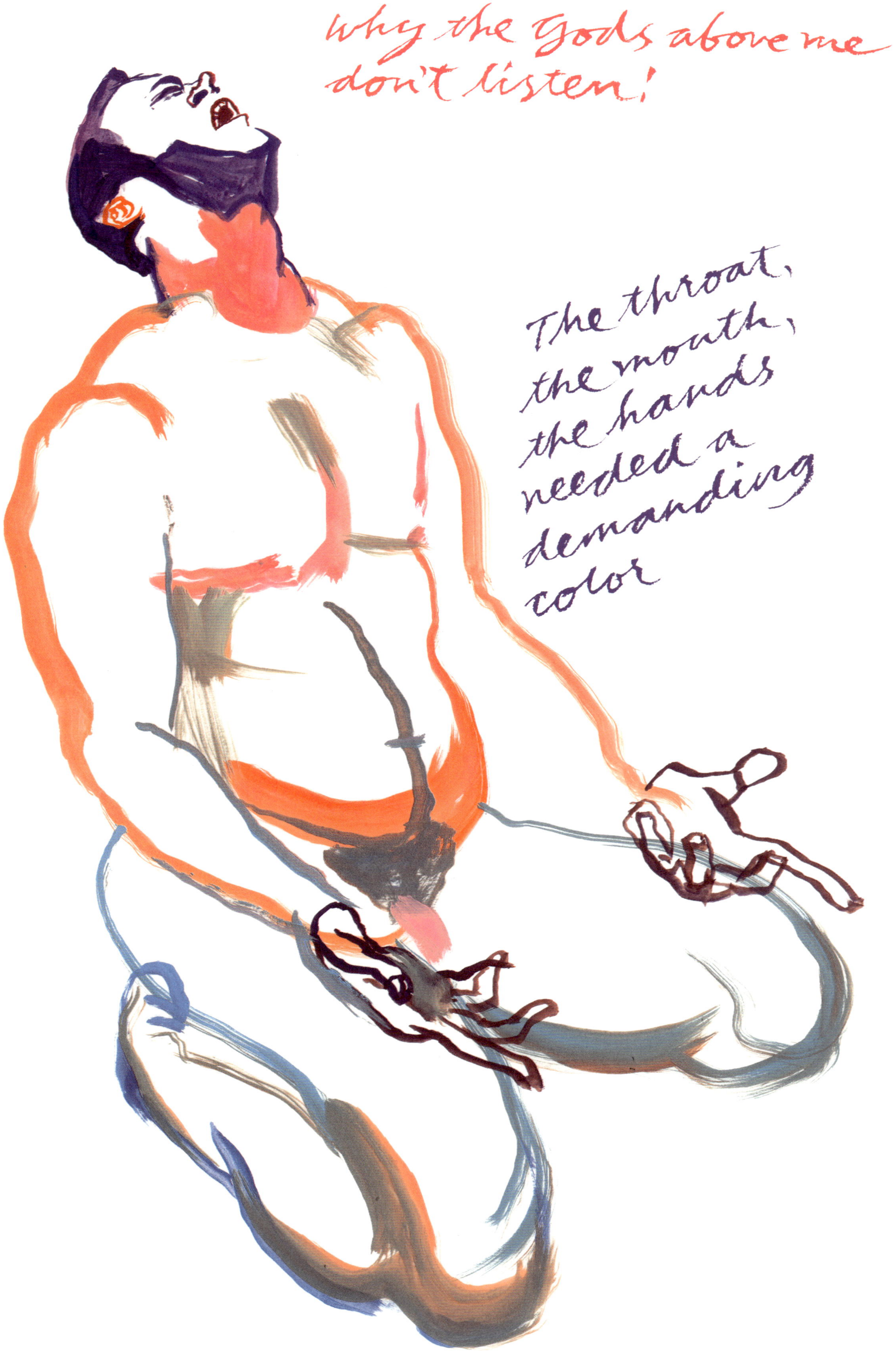

why the Gods above me
don't listen!

The throat,
the mouth,
the hands
needed a
demanding
color

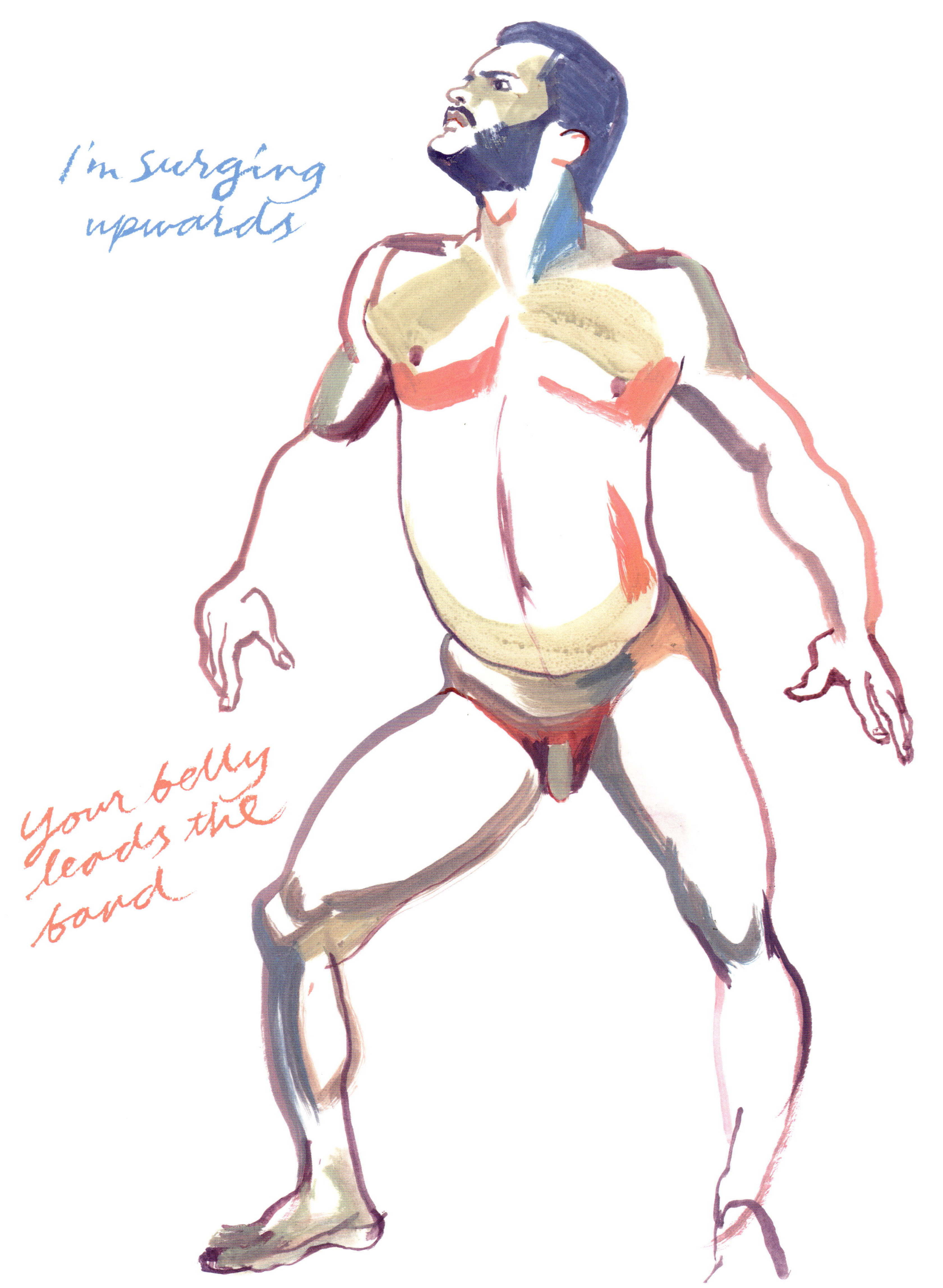

I'm surging
upwards

Your belly
leads the
band

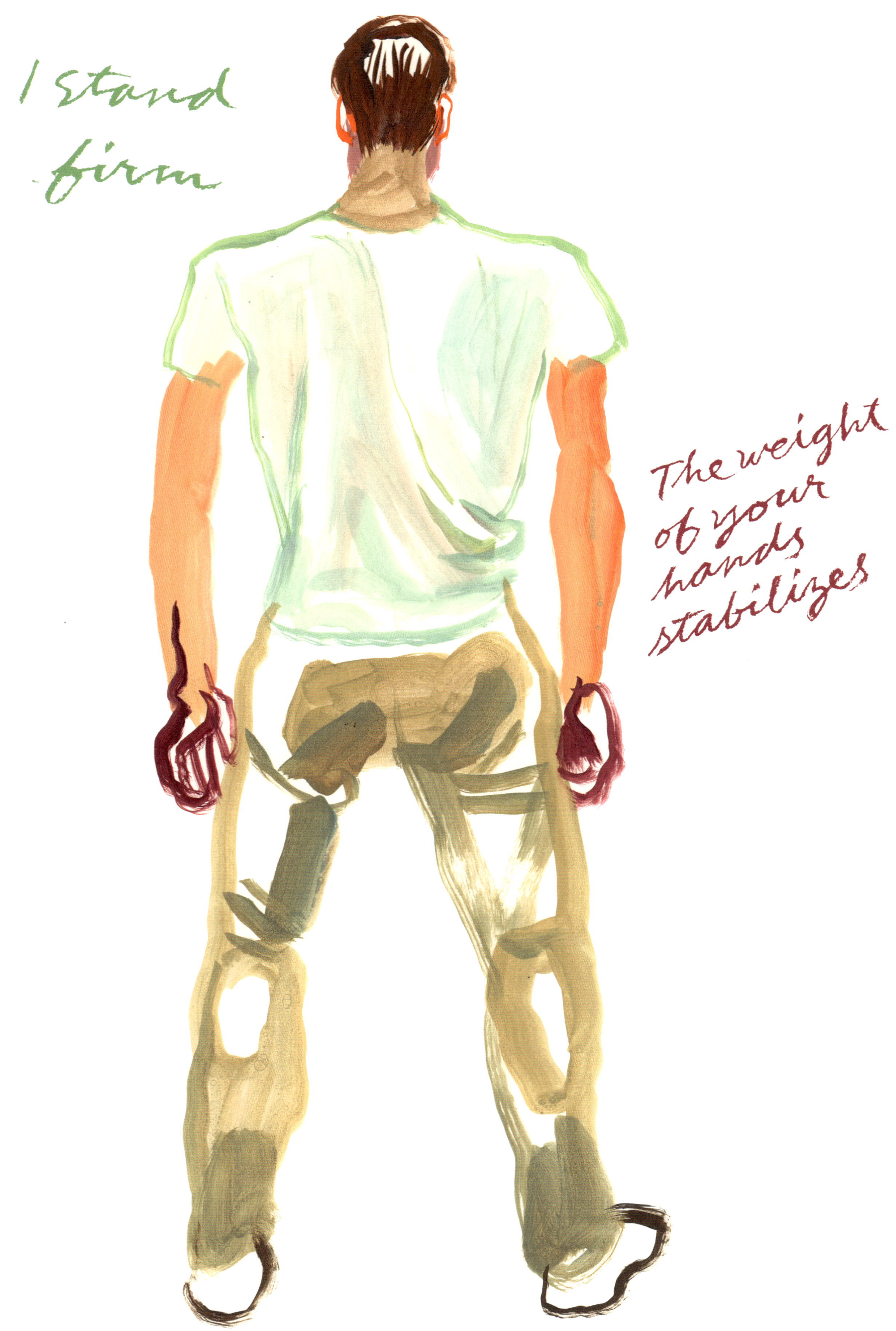

I stand
firm

The weight
of your
hands
stabilizes

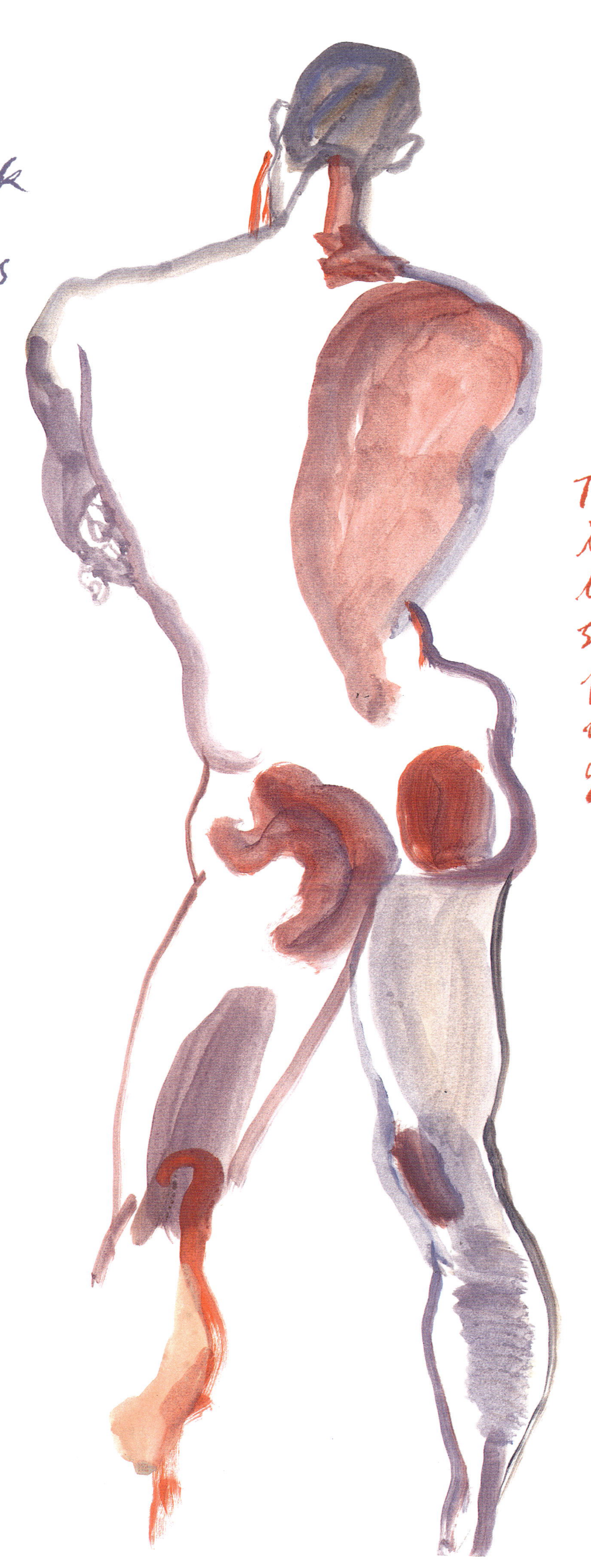

My hand
on my cheek
feels like
it connects
to the
pressure
in my leg

The big push
in your
buttocks
sets up the
flowing
arc of
your back

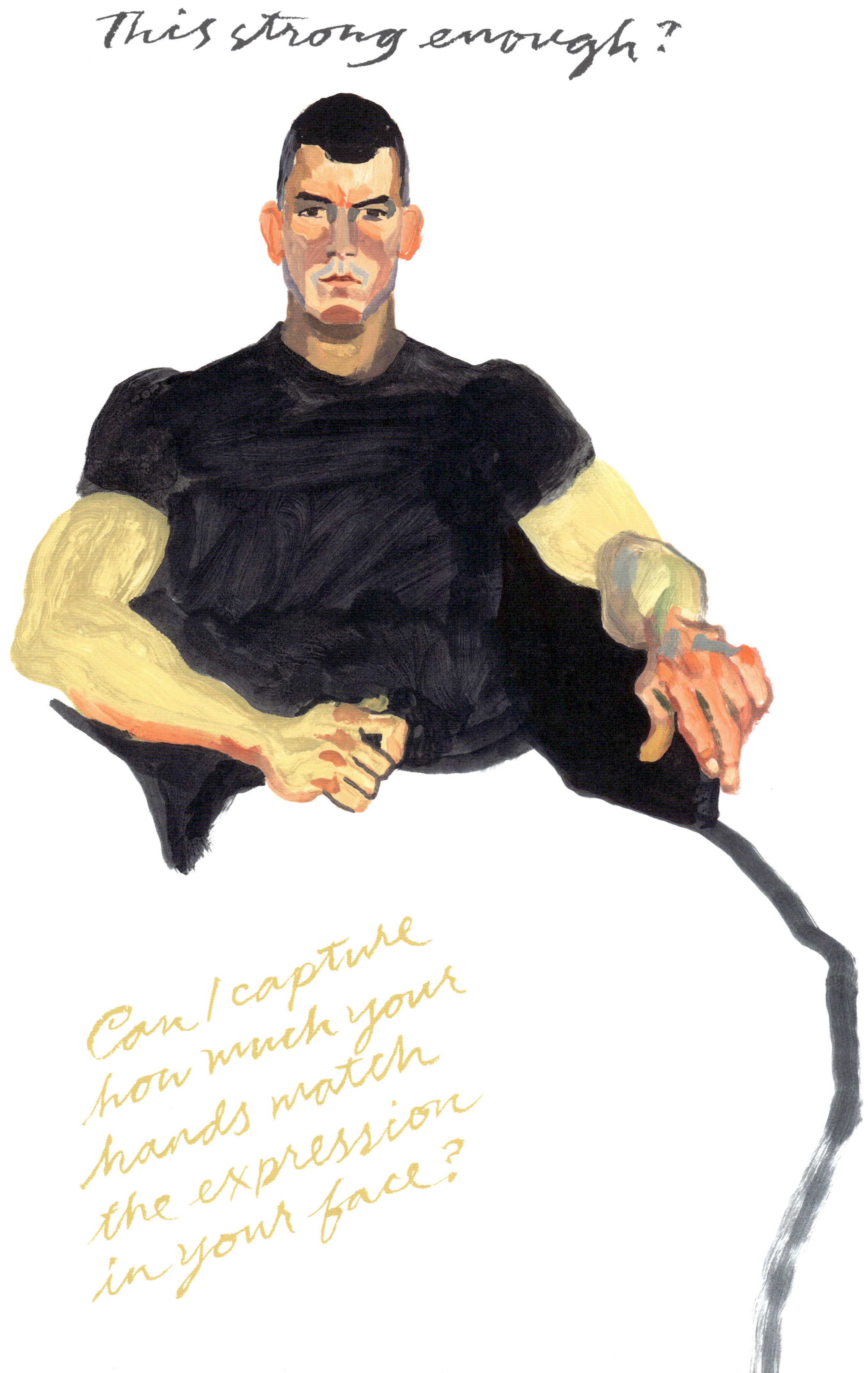

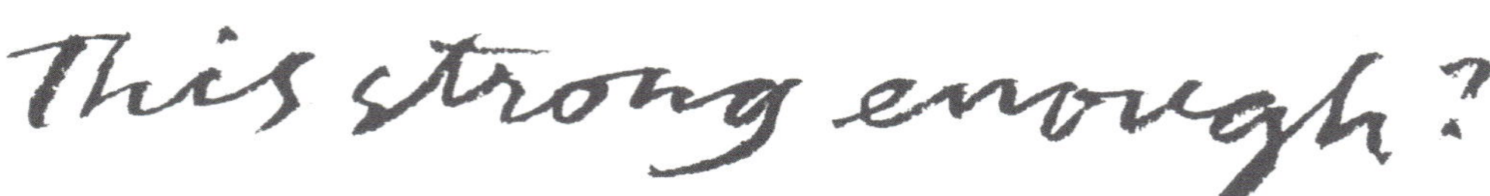

Can I capture
how much your
hands match
the expression
in your face?

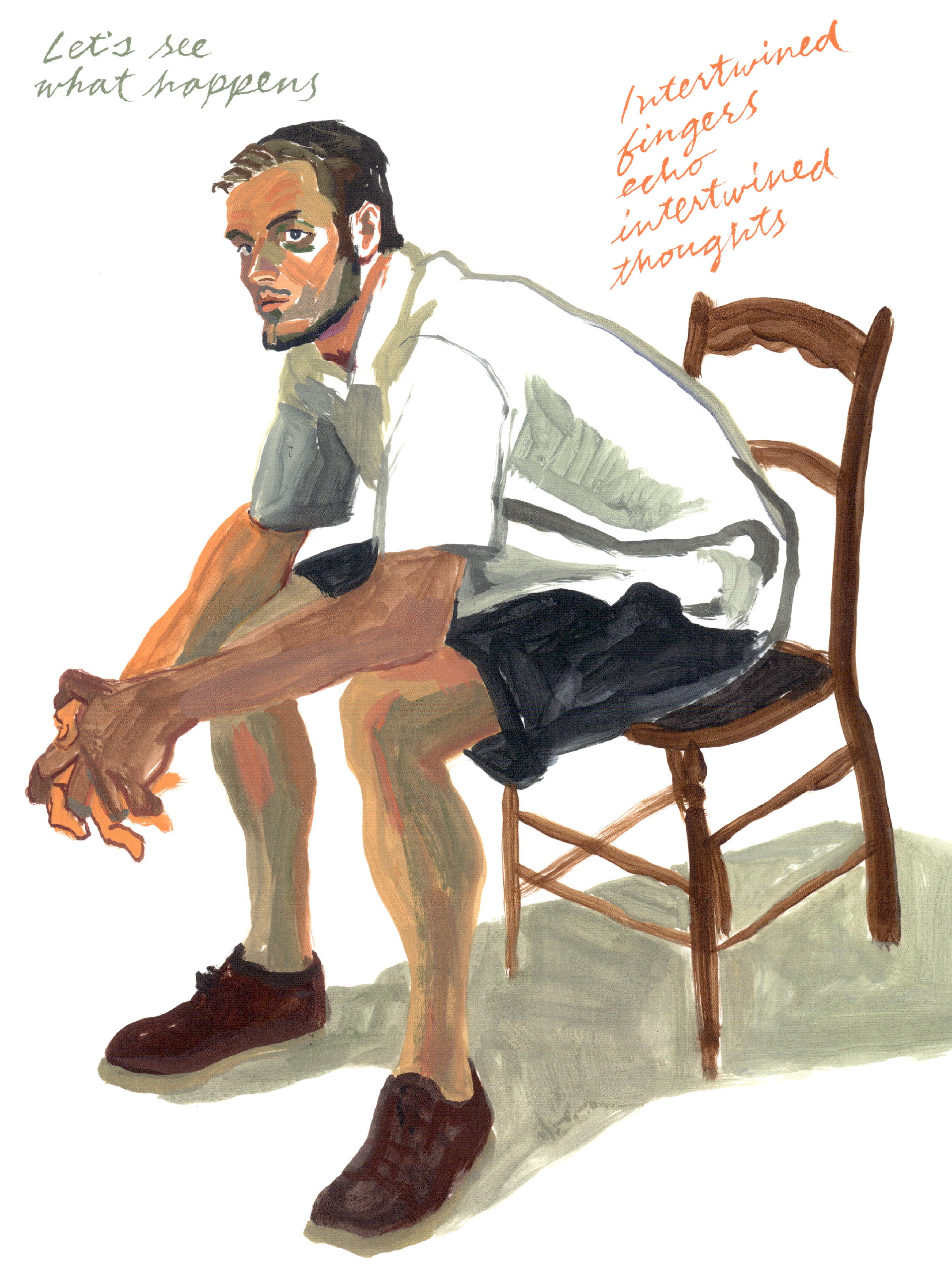
Let's see
what happens
intertwined
fingers
echo
intertwined
thoughts

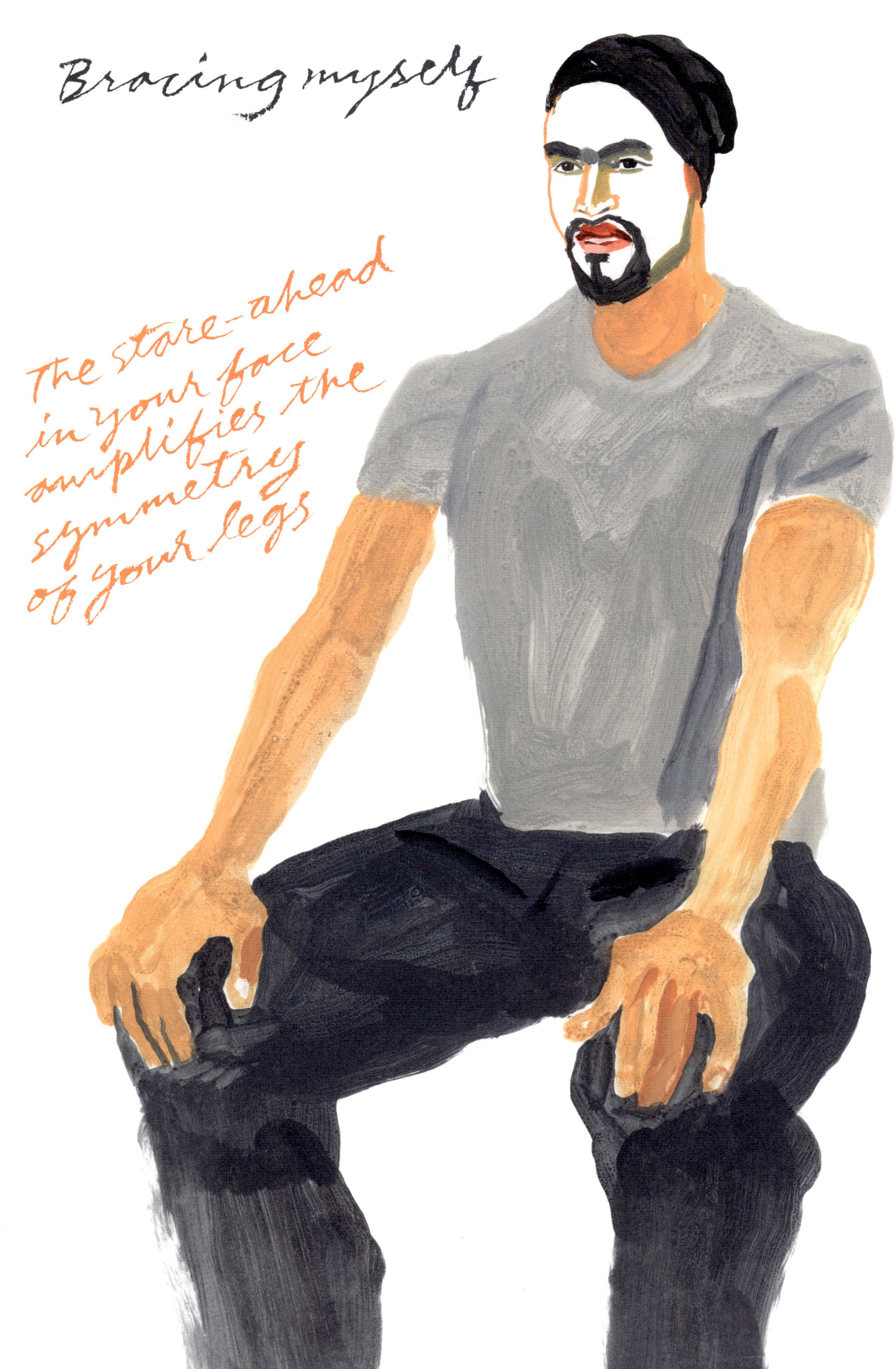

Bracing myself

The stare-ahead
in your face
amplifies the
symmetry
of your legs

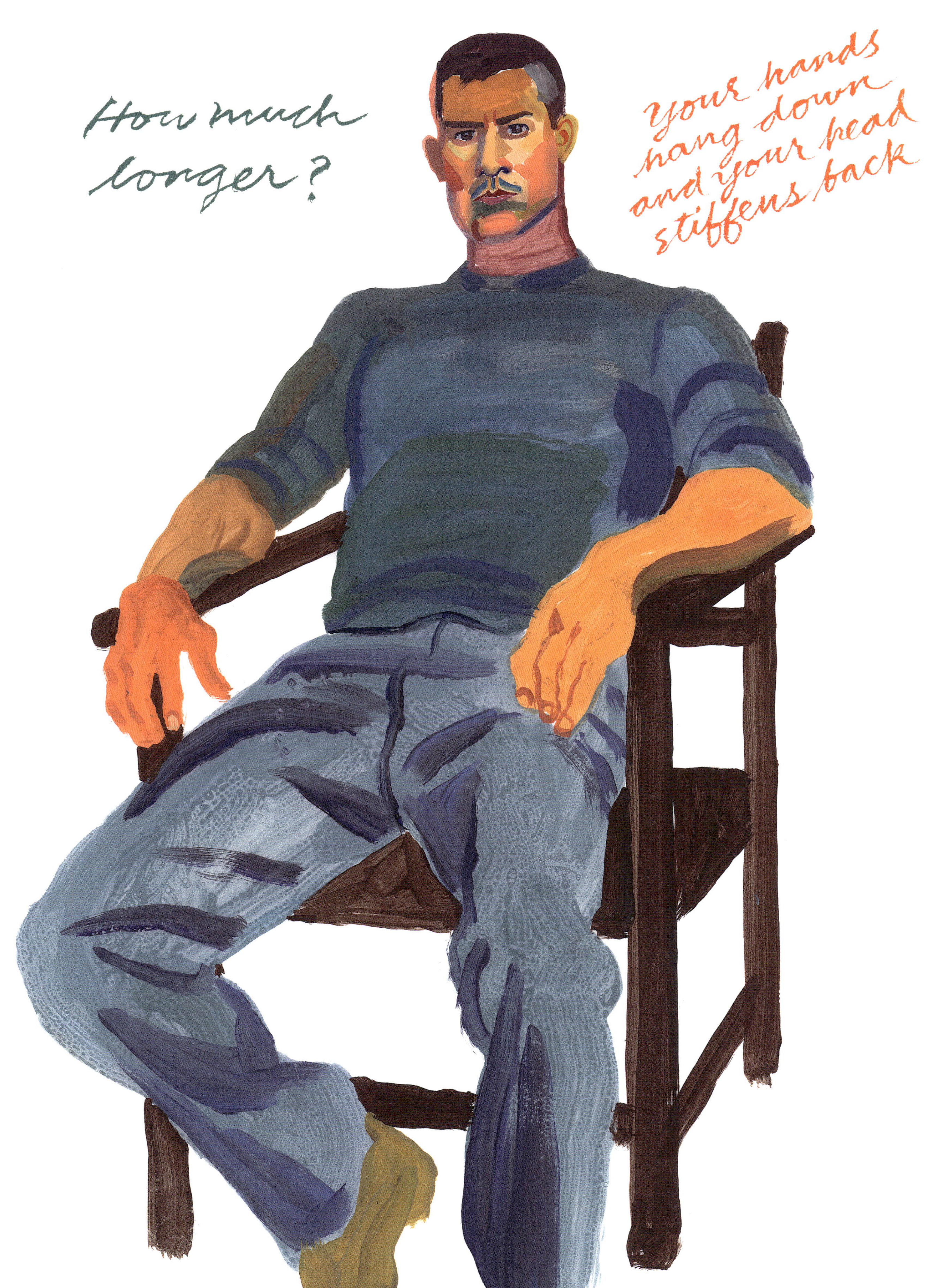

How much longer?
Your hands hang down and your head stiffens back

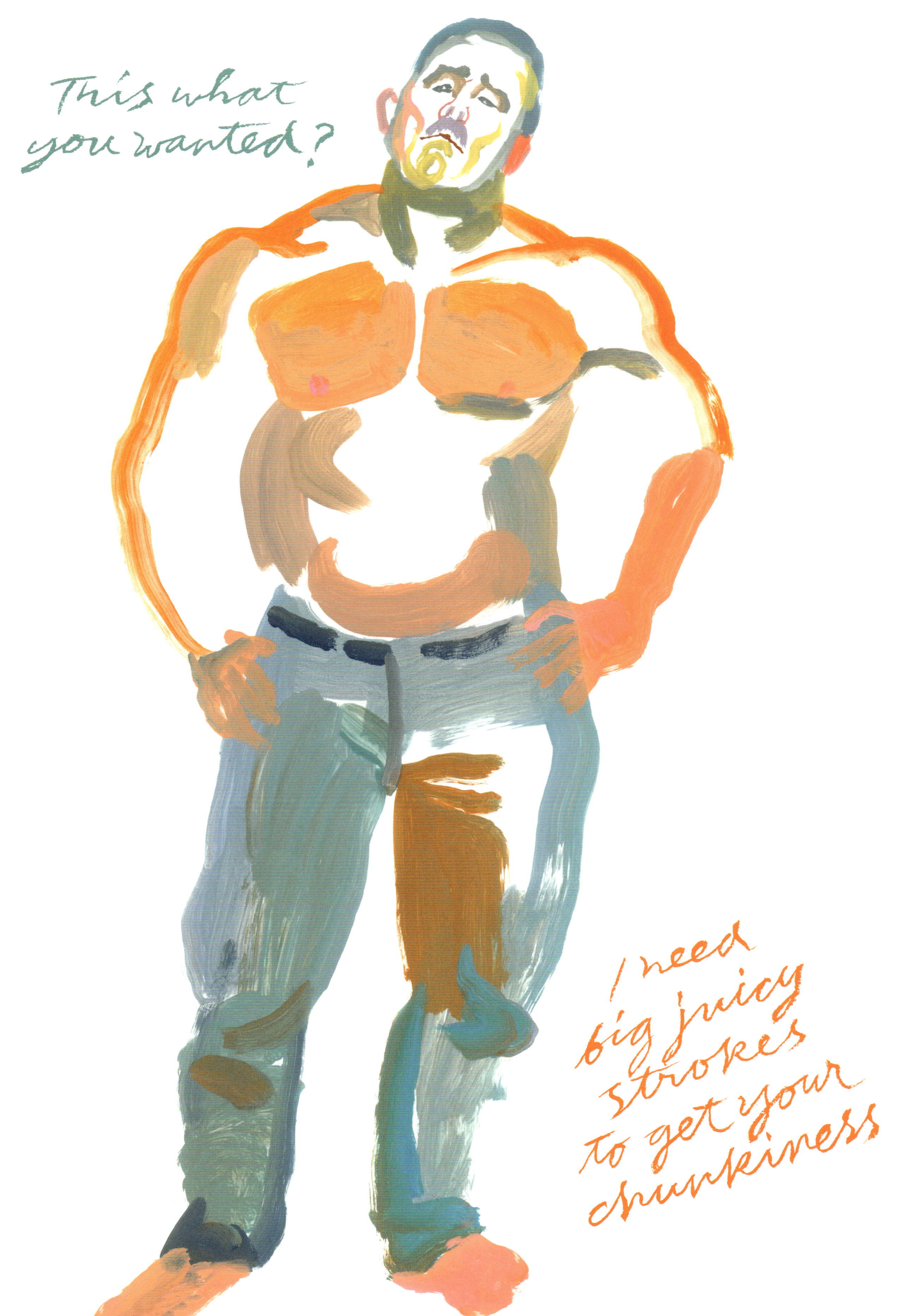

This what
you wanted?
I need
big juicy
strokes
to get your
chunkiness

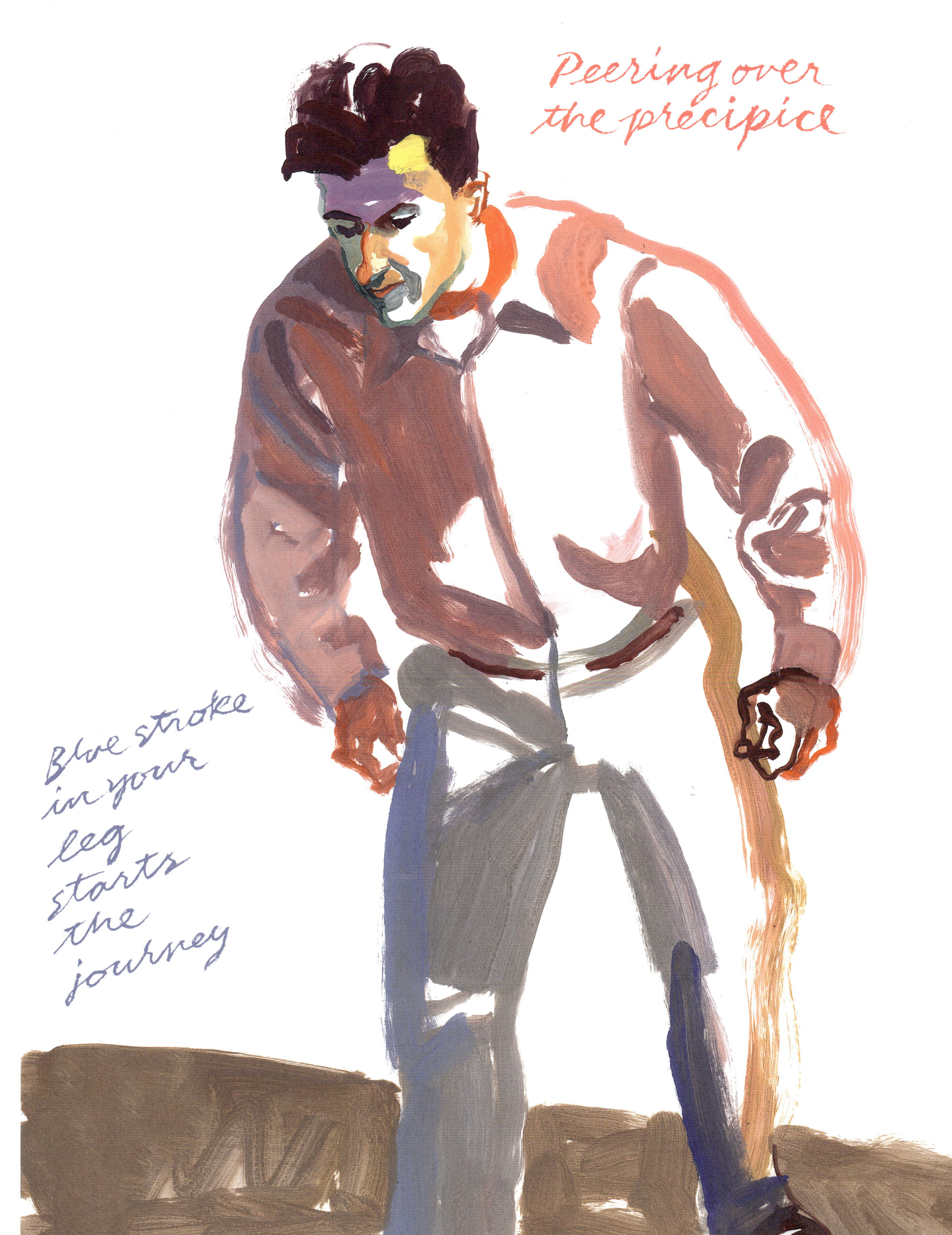

Peering over
the precipice

Blue stroke
in your
leg
starts
the
journey

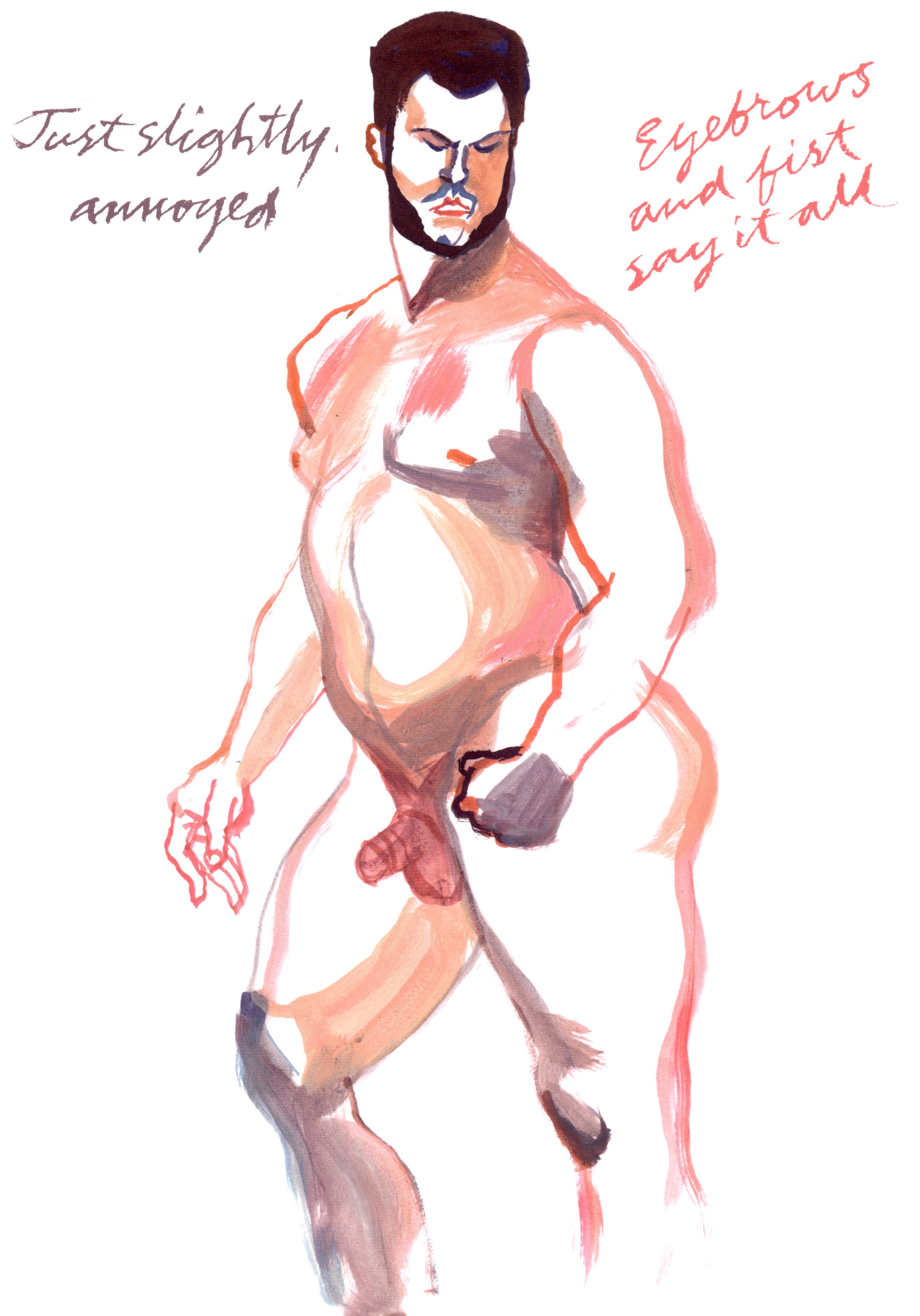

Just slightly.
annoyed
Eyebrows
and fist
say it all

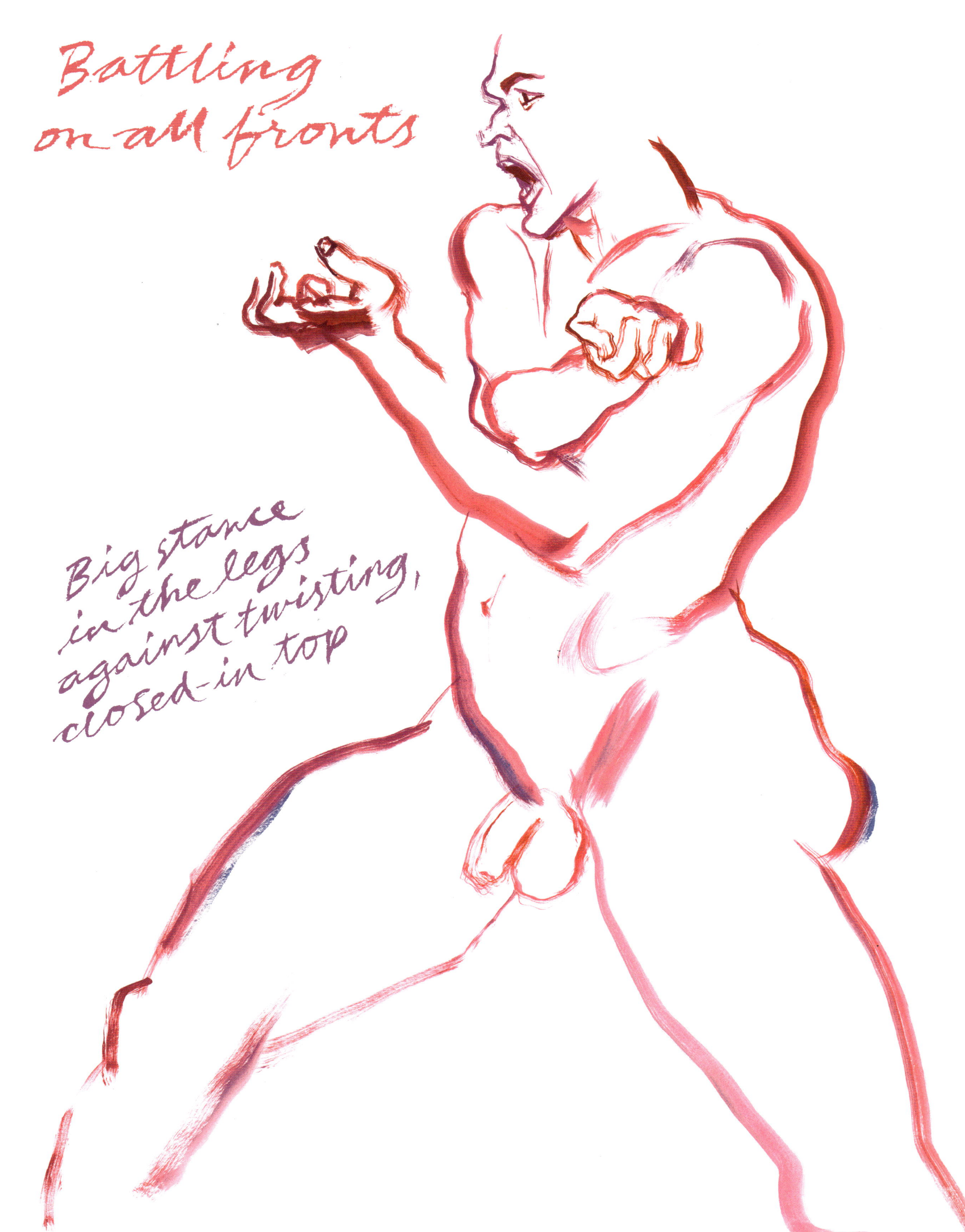

Battling
on all fronts
Big stance
in the legs
against twisting,
closed-in top

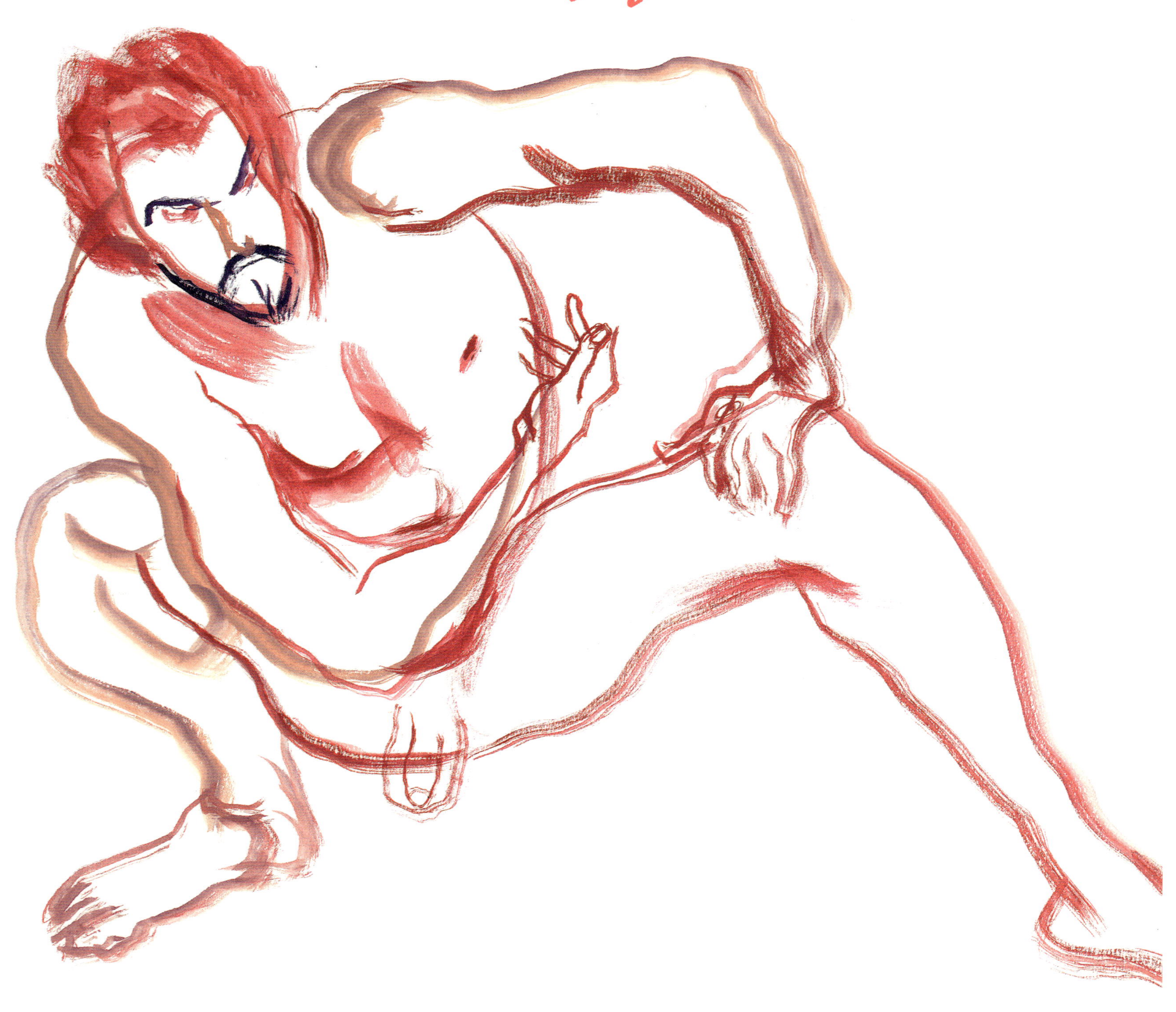
I'm packed
with power

Fast moving lines
to suggest the
squatting is about
to change
any minute

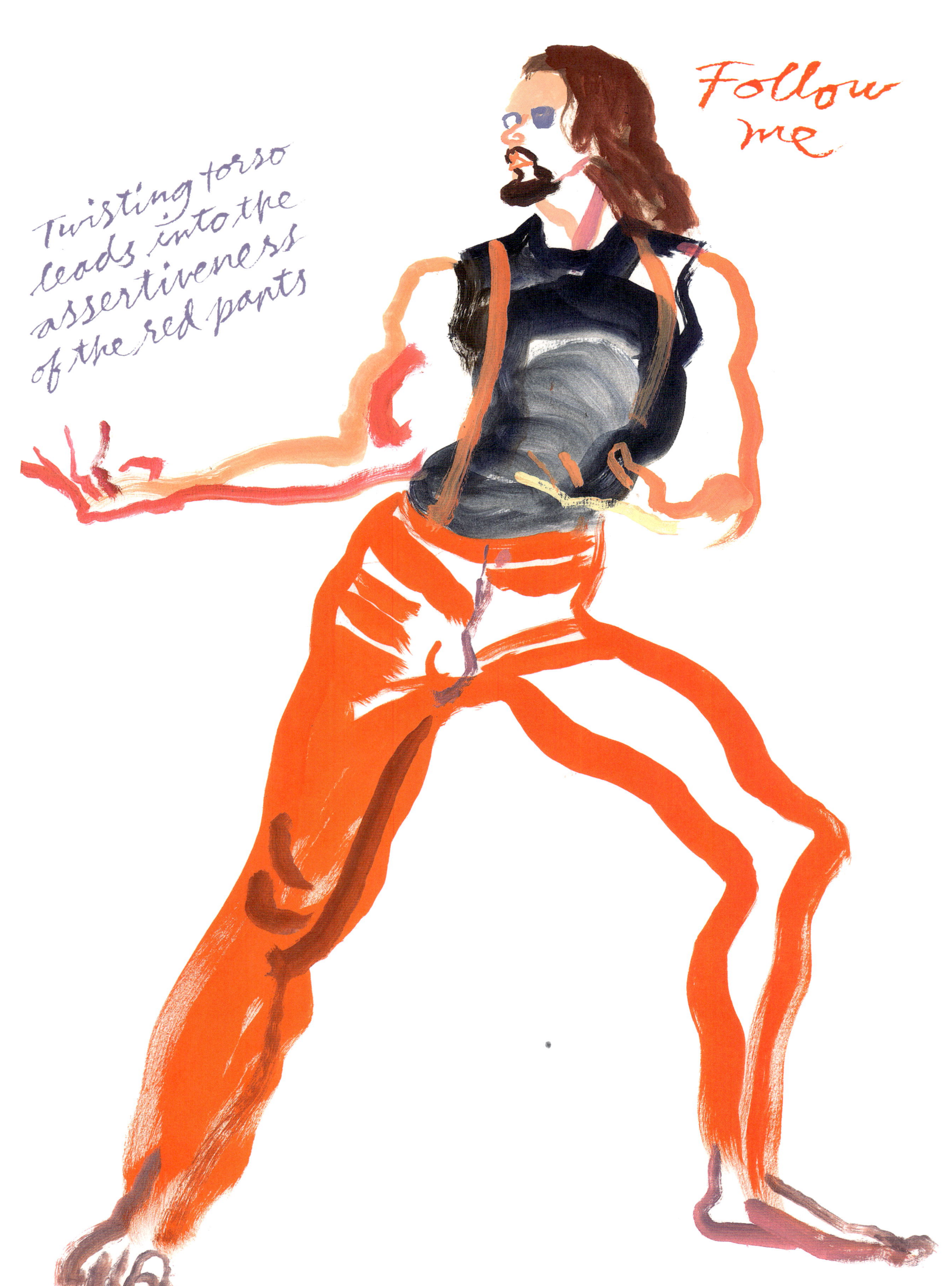

Twisting torso
leads into the
assertiveness
of the red pants

Follow
me

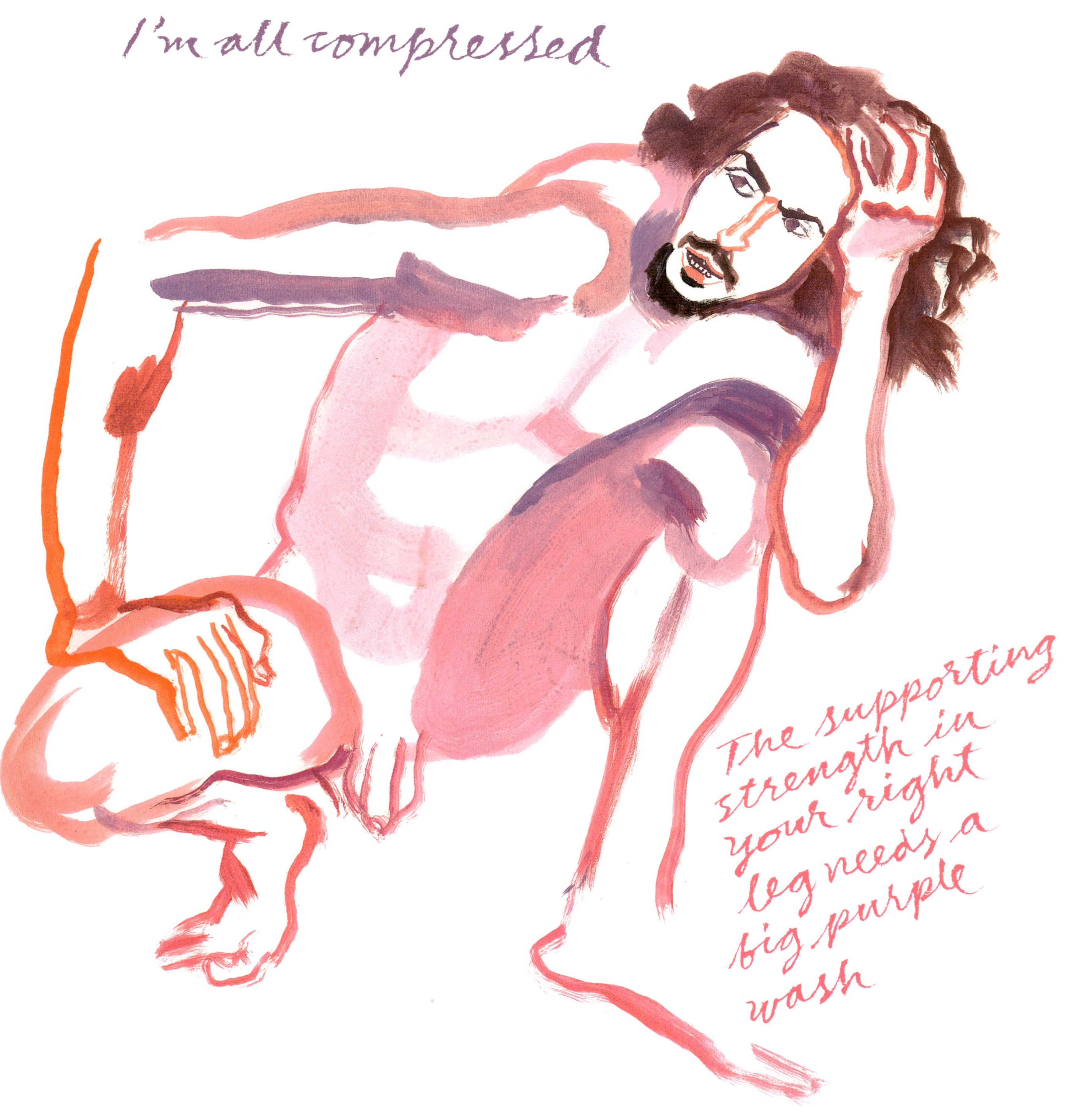
I'm all compressed
The supporting strength in your right leg needs a big purple wash

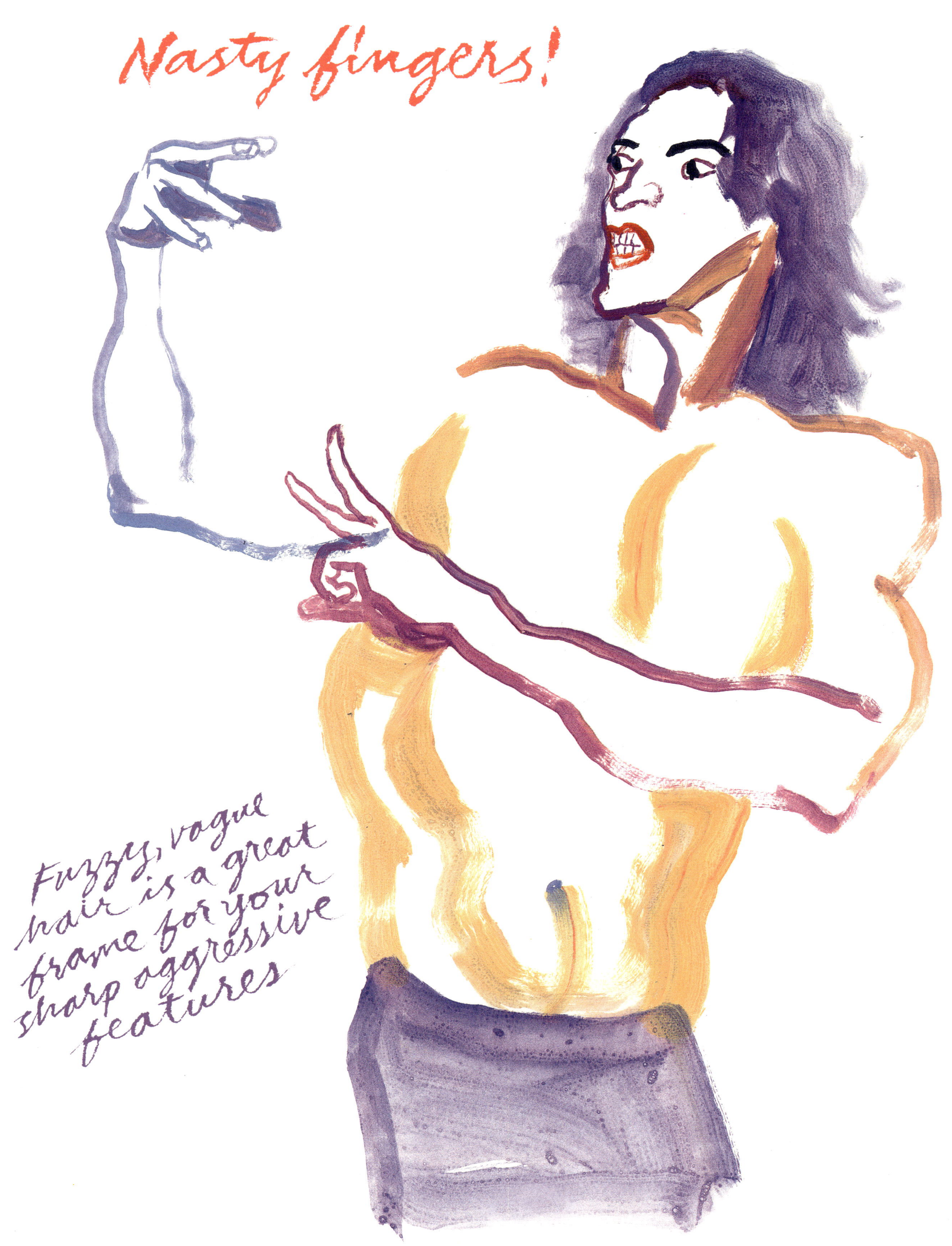

Nasty fingers!
Fuzzy, vague hair is a great frame for your sharp aggressive features

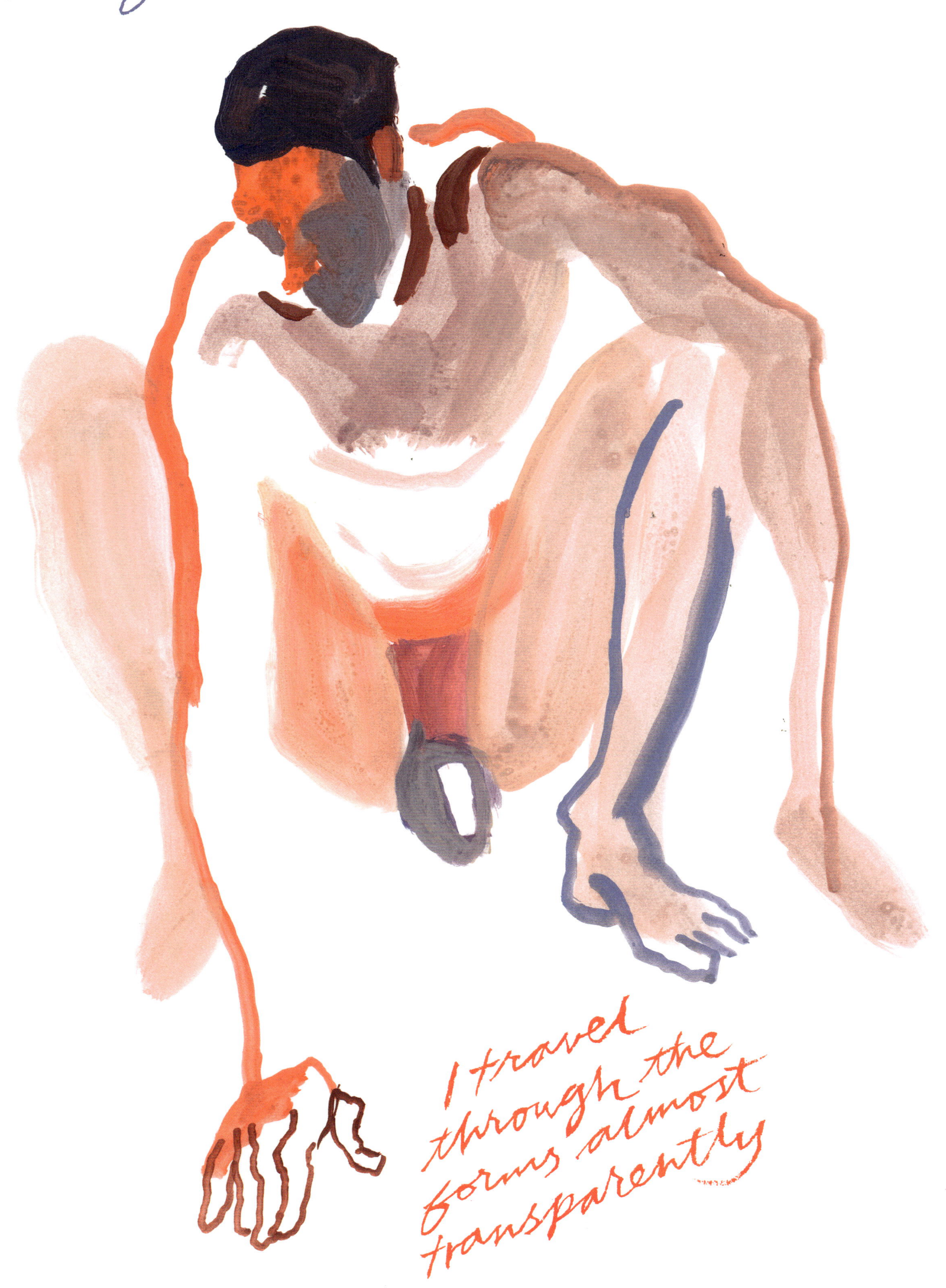

Feet and fingers
feel the floor

I travel
through the
forms almost
transparently

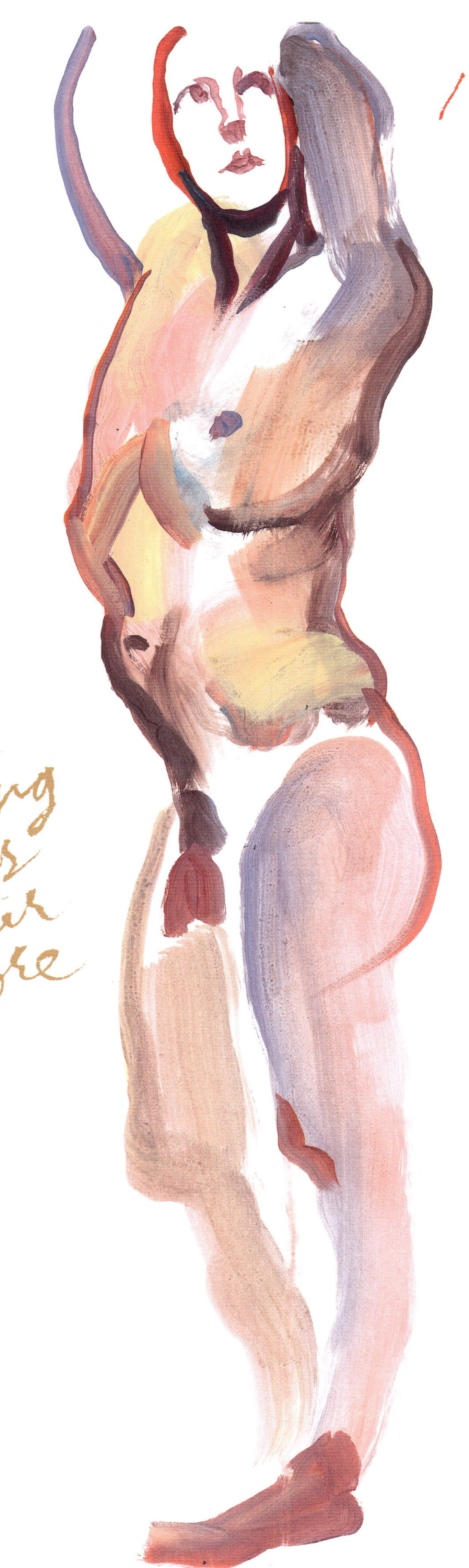

I feel like
a Greek
column

I paint
a unifying
softness
over your
strong core

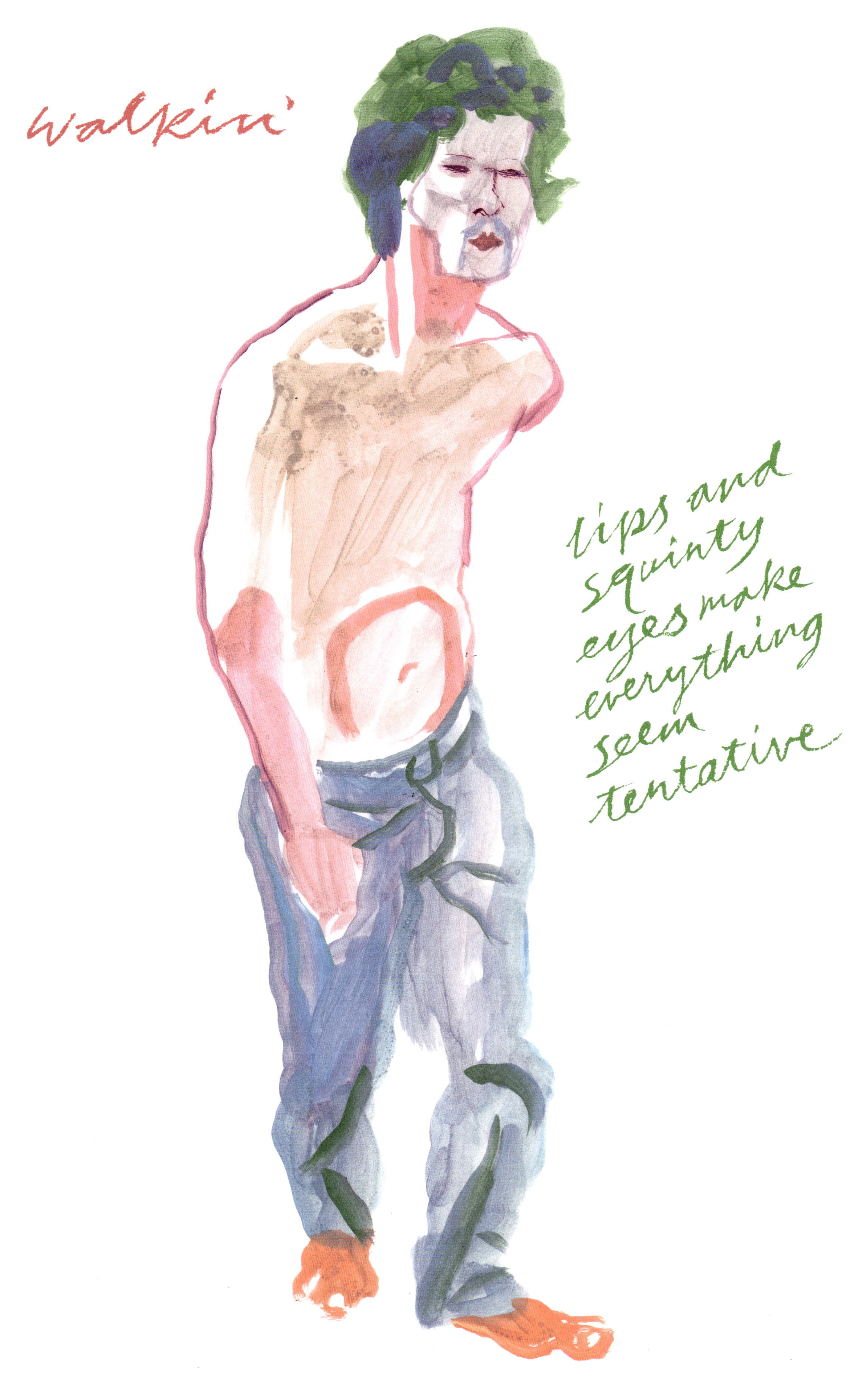

walkin'
lips and squinty eyes make everything seem tentative

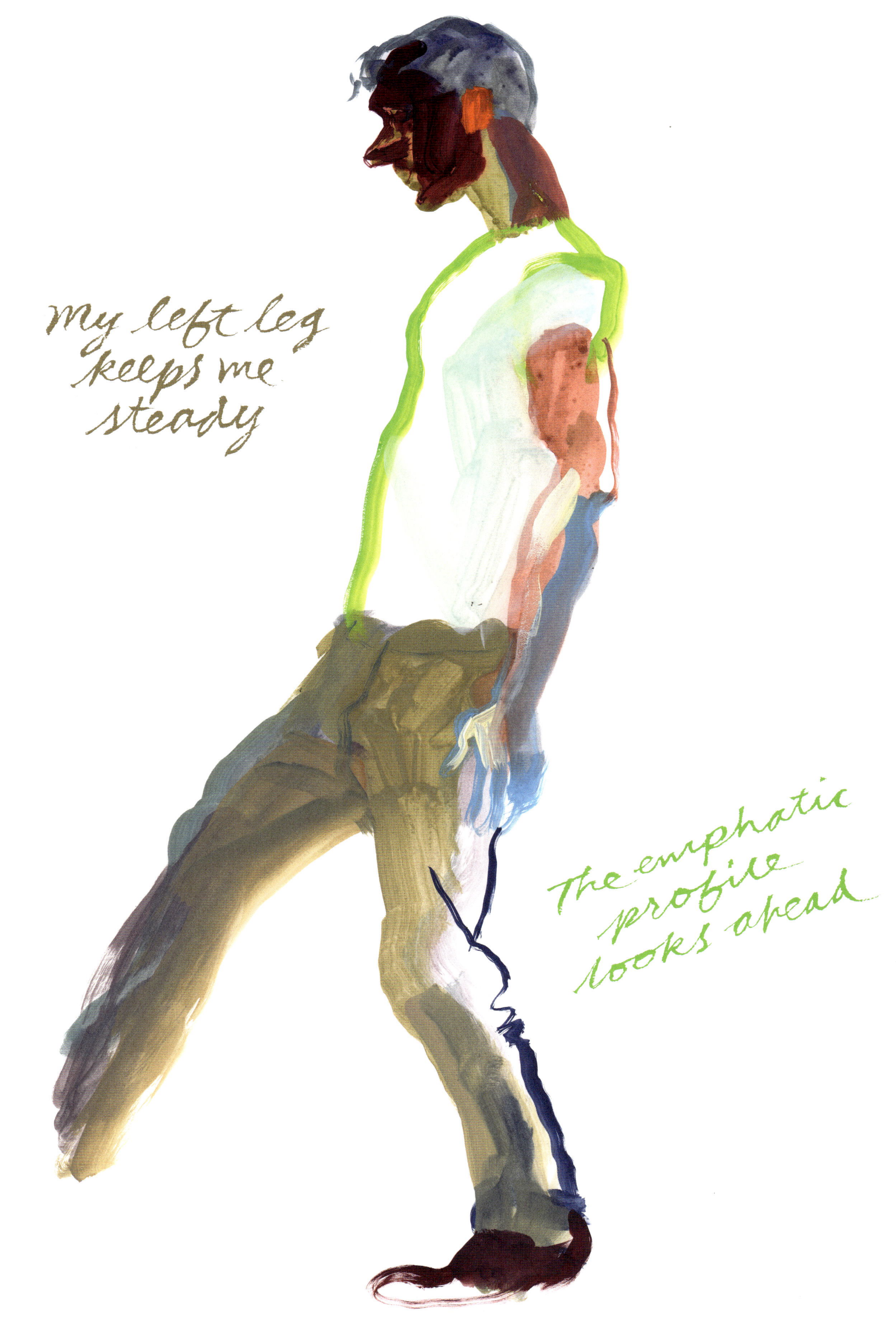
my left leg
keeps me
steady
The emphatic
profile
looks ahead

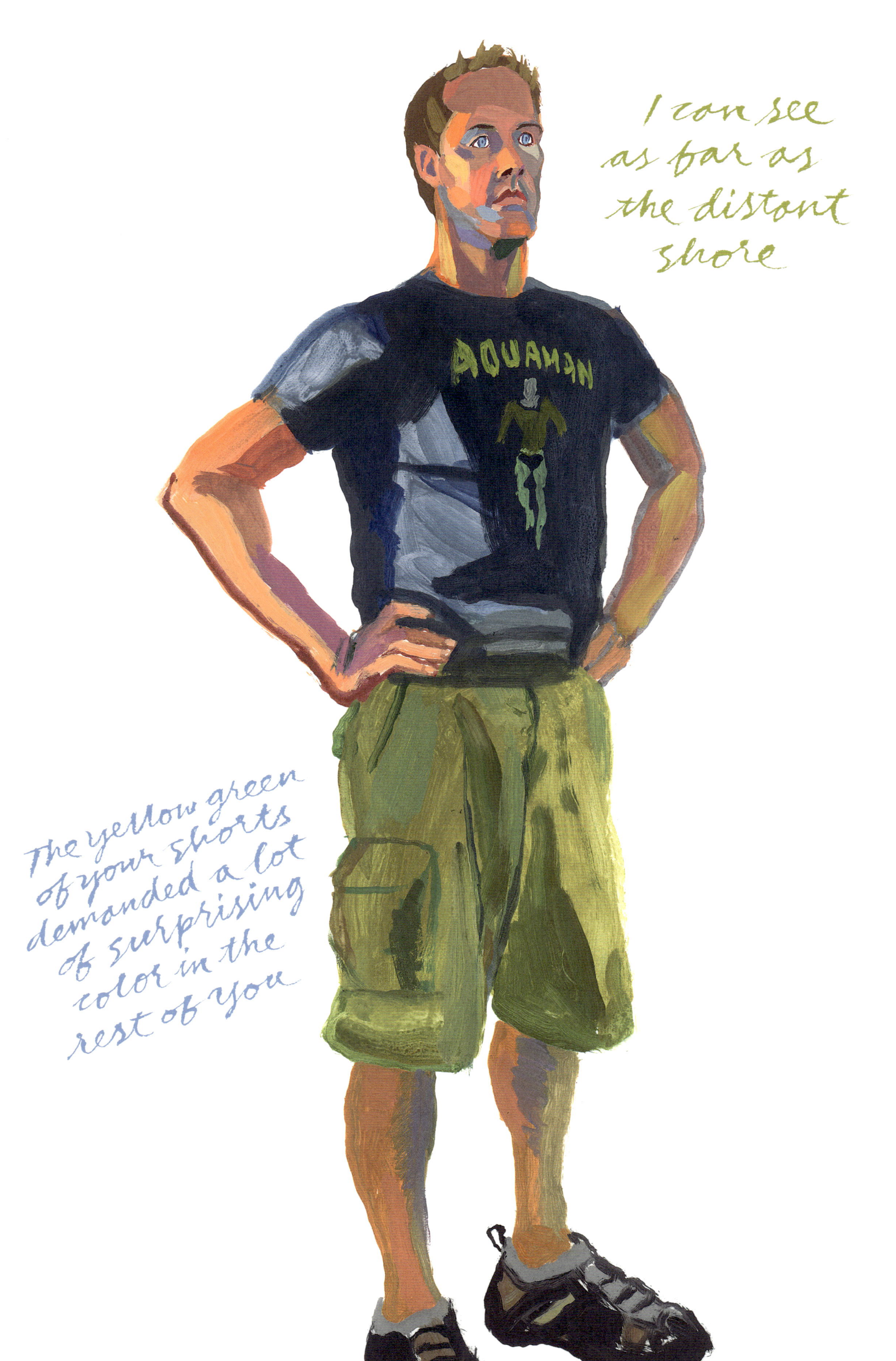
AQUAMAN

I can see
as far as
the distant
shore

The yellow green
of your shorts
demanded a lot
of surprising
color in the
rest of you

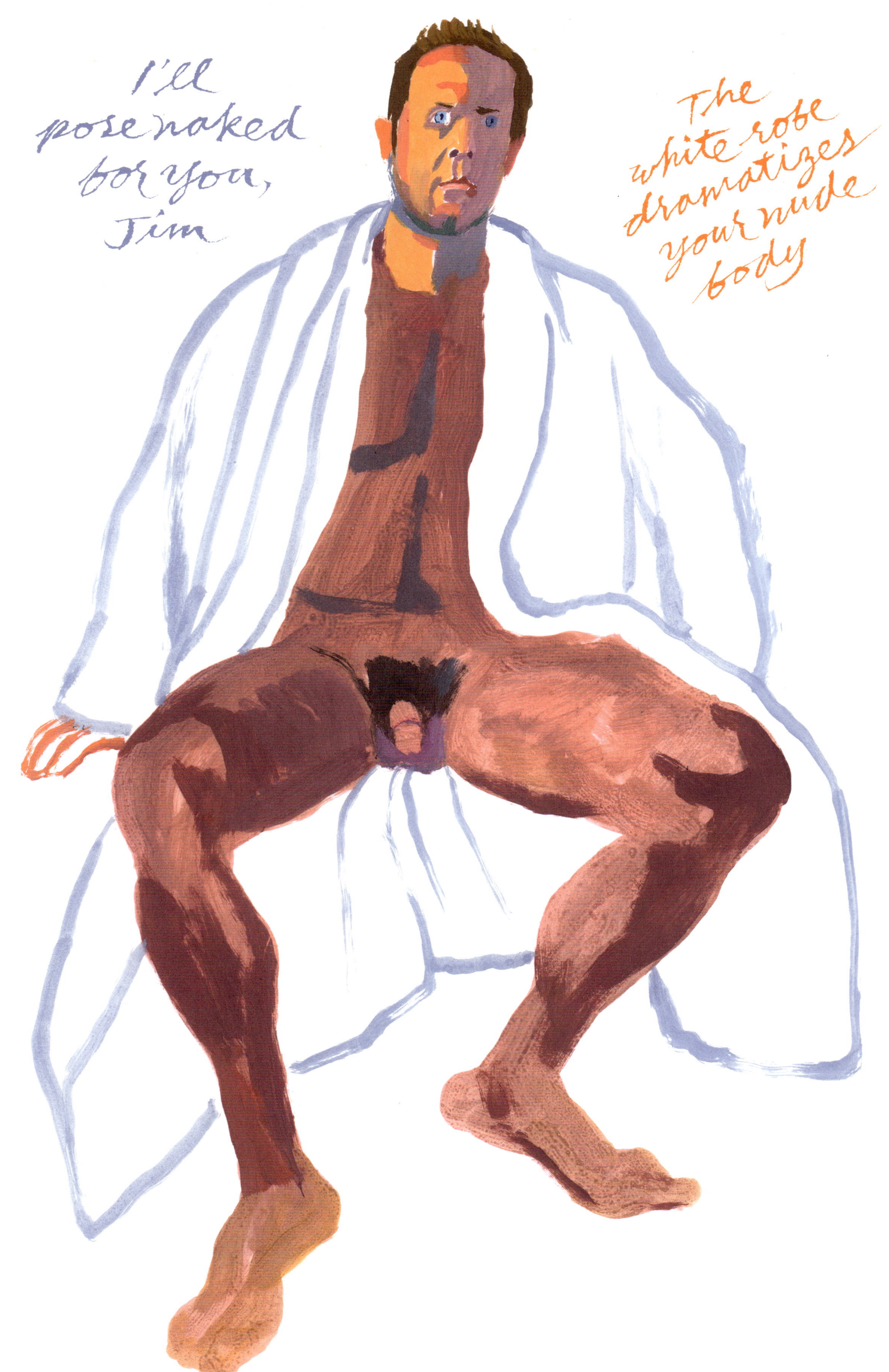

I'll pose naked for you, Jim
The white robe dramatizes your nude body

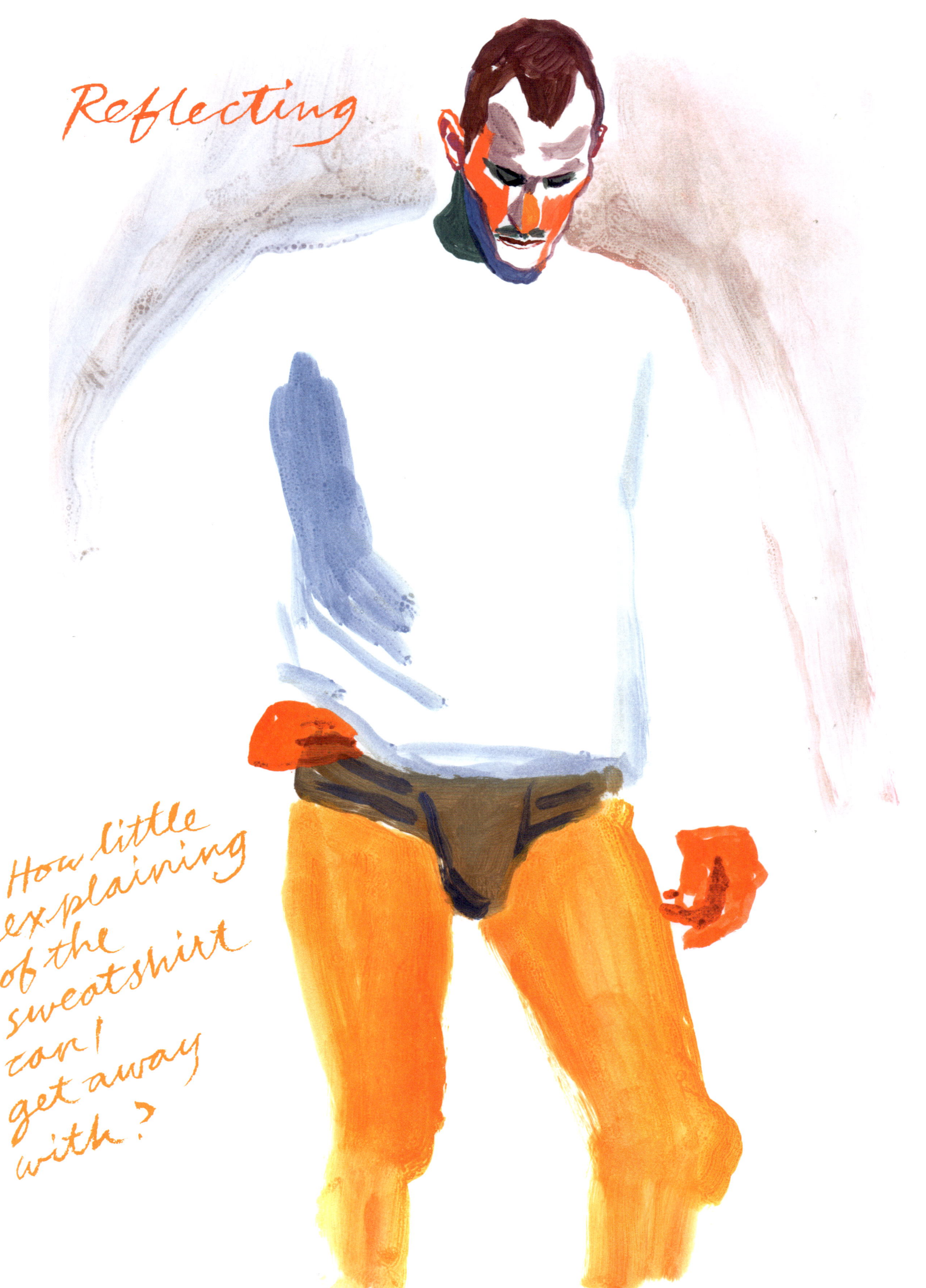

Reflecting

How little
explaining
of the
sweatshirt
can I
get away
with ?

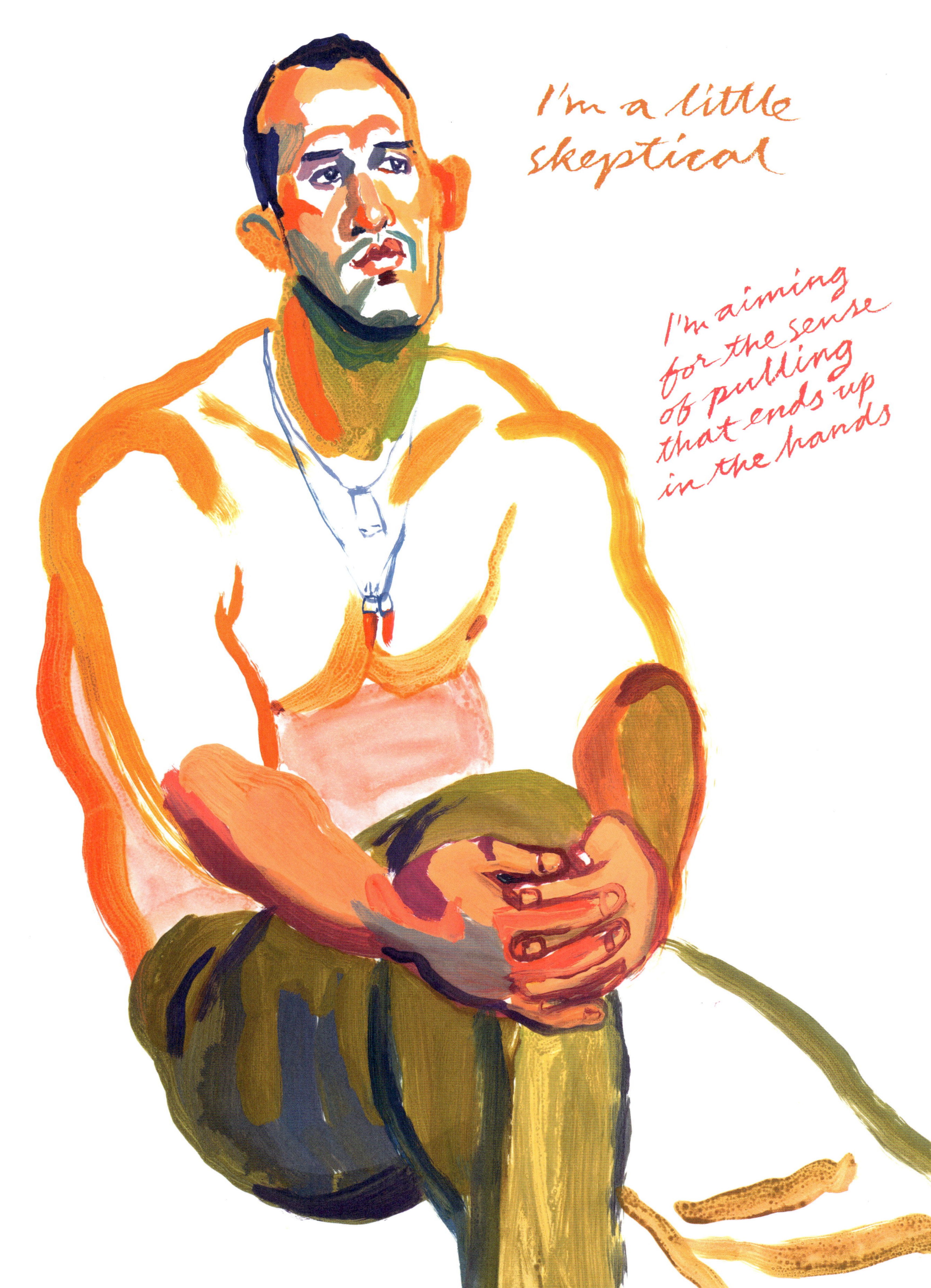
I'm a little skeptical
I'm aiming for the sense of pulling that ends up in the hands

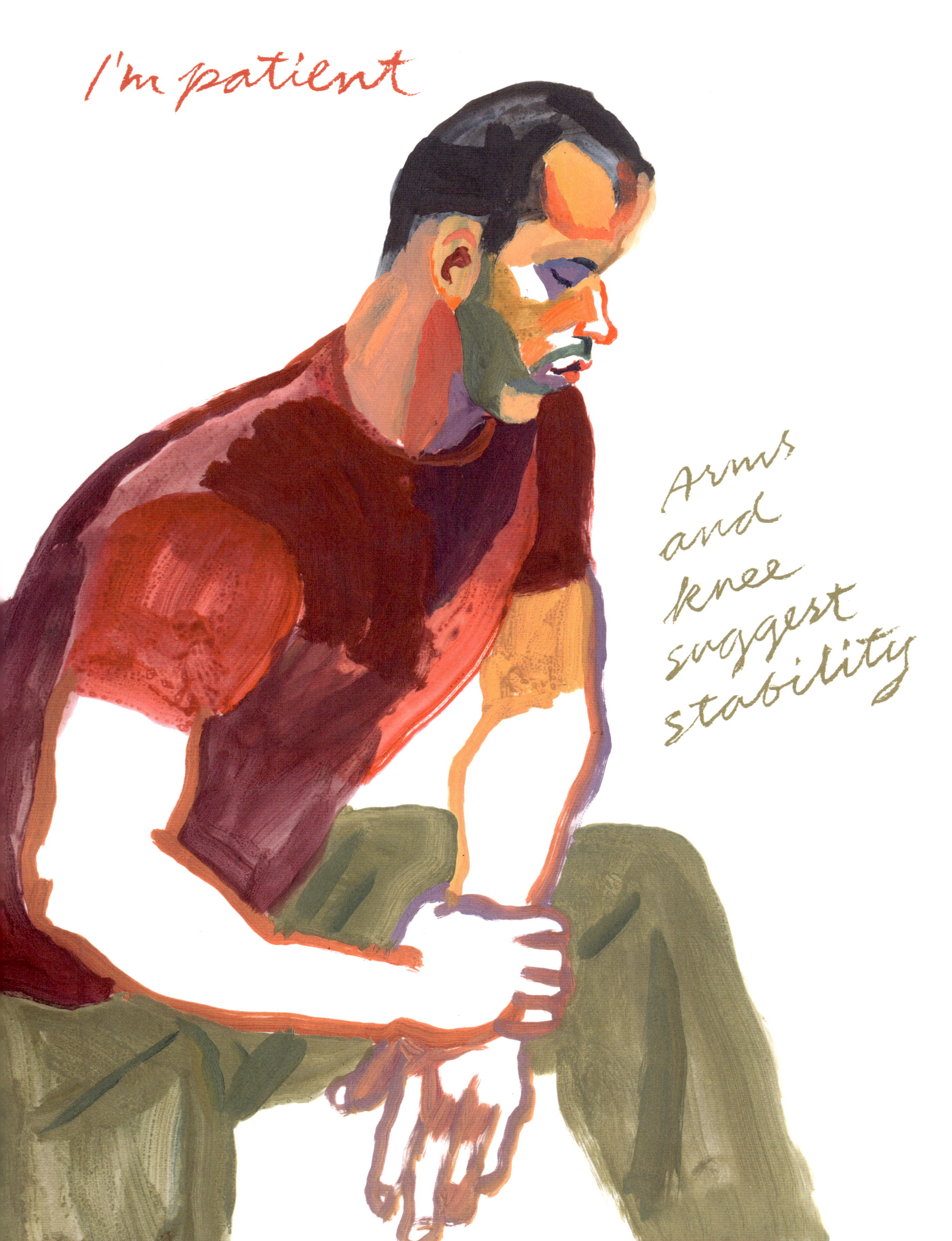
I'm patient
Arms and knee suggest stability

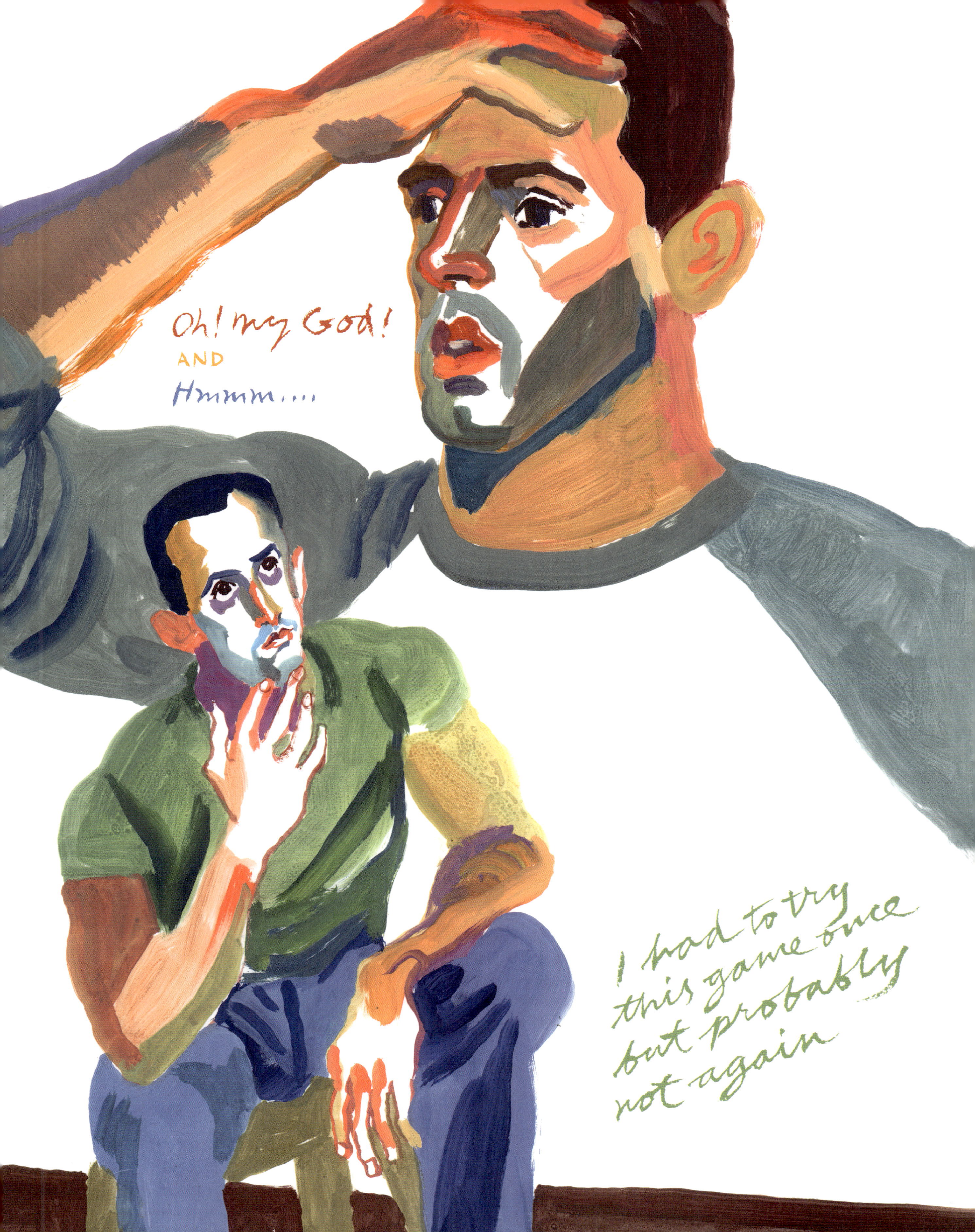

Oh! my God!
AND
Hmmm....
I had to try
this game once
but probably
not again

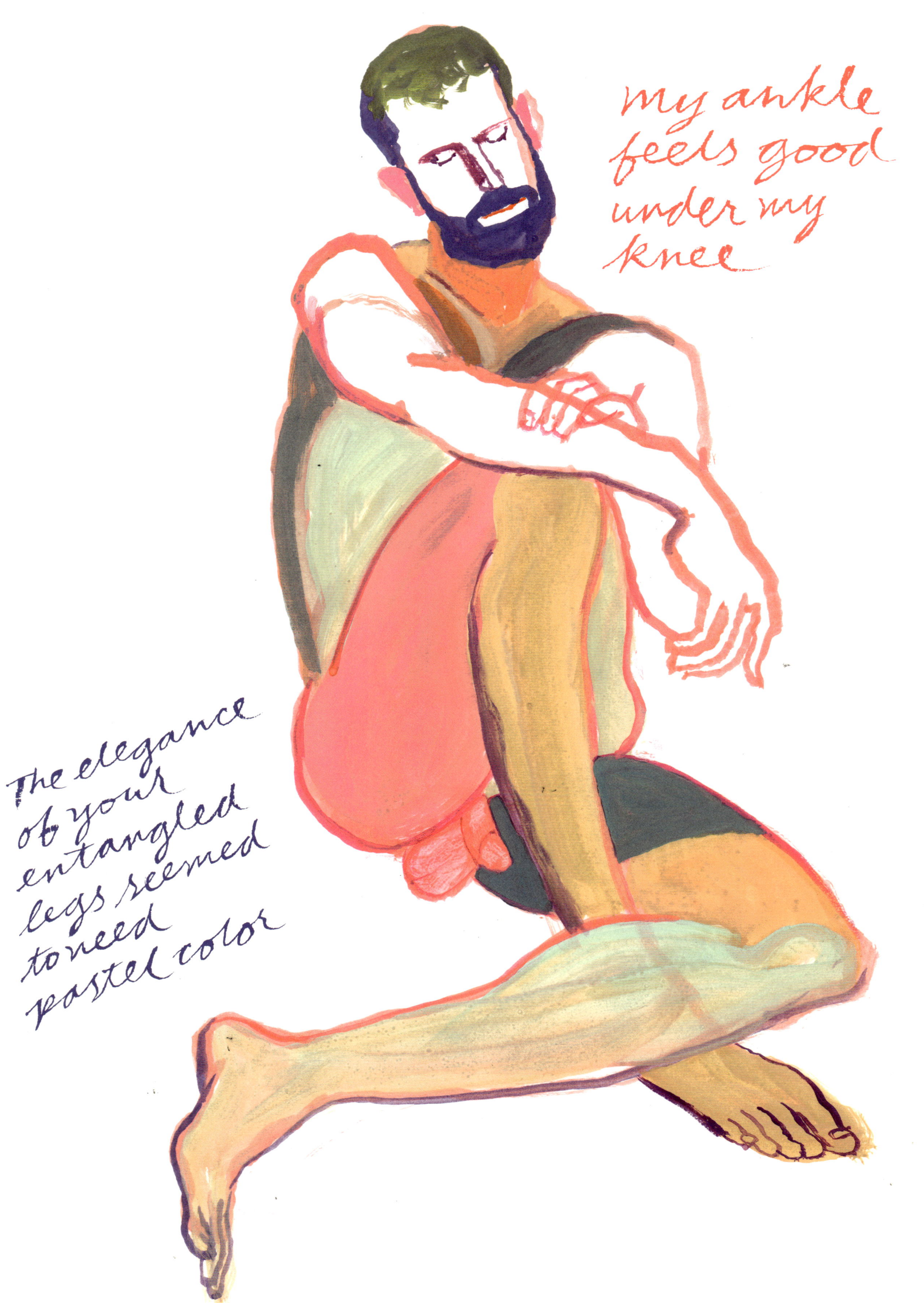
my ankle
feels good
under my
knee

The elegance
of your
entangled
legs seemed
to need
pastel color

What's up there?
Your face and hands suggest an imminent moment

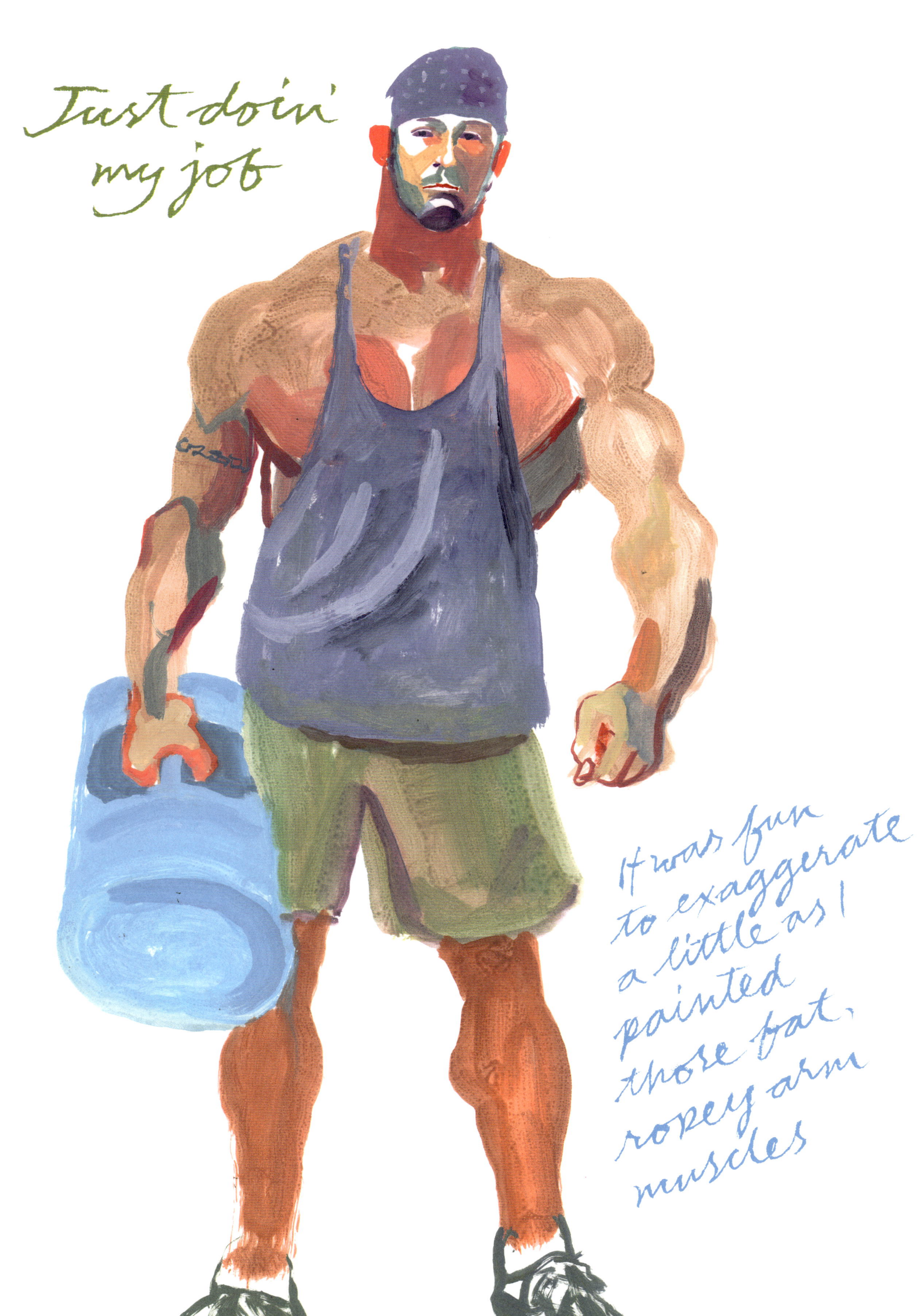

Just doin'
my job

It was fun
to exaggerate
a little as I
painted
those fat,
ropey arm
muscles

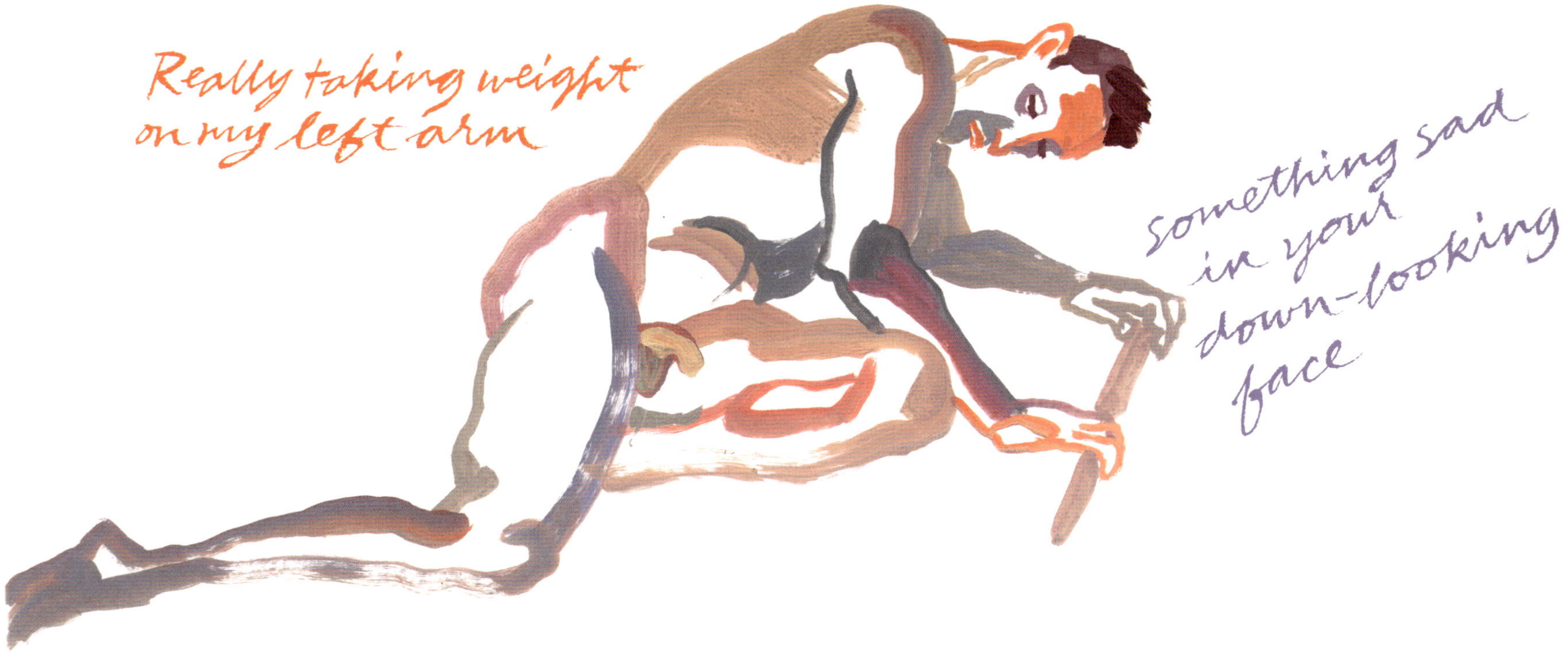

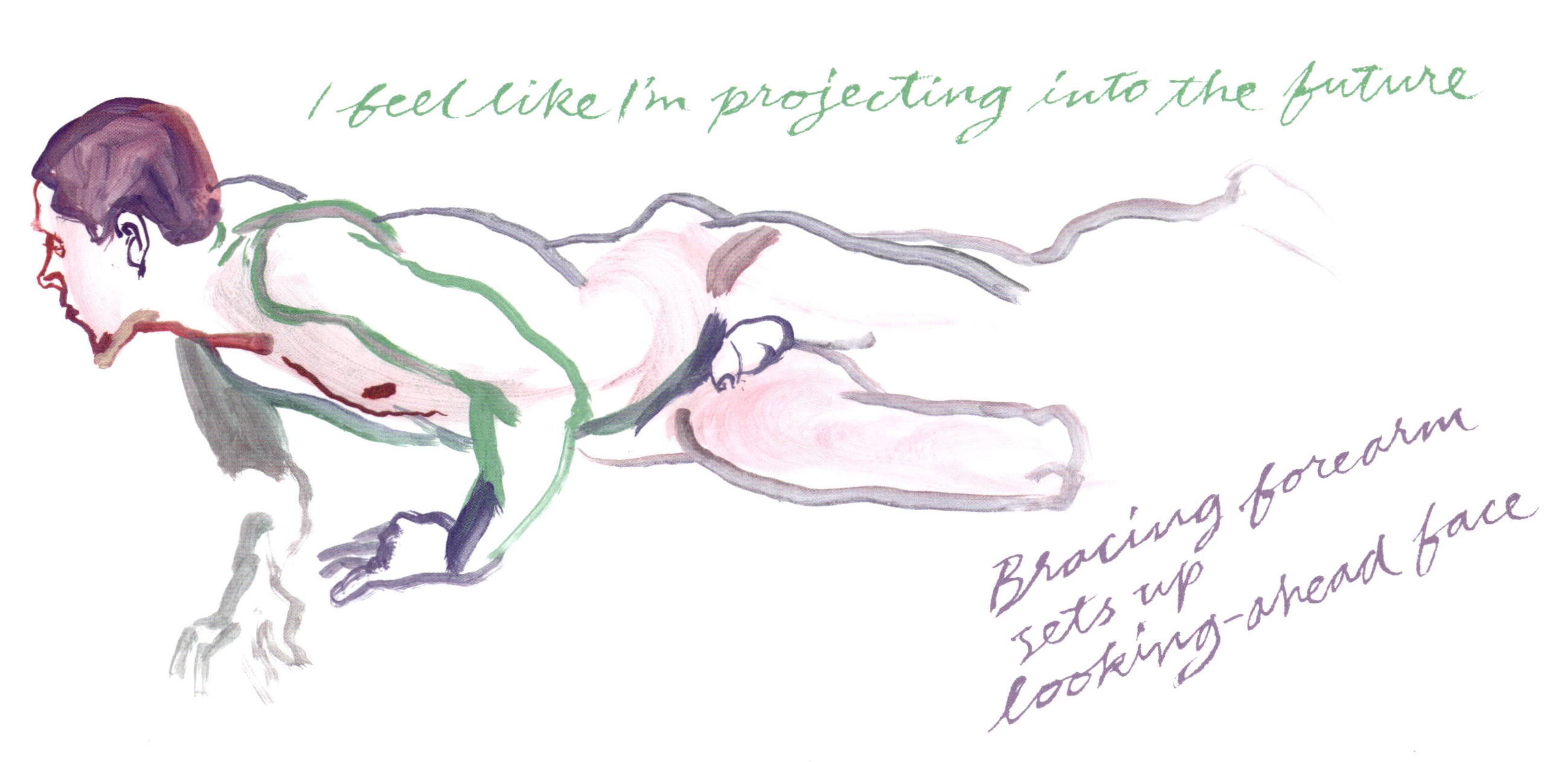
Really taking weight on my left arm
something sad in your down-looking face
This feels good 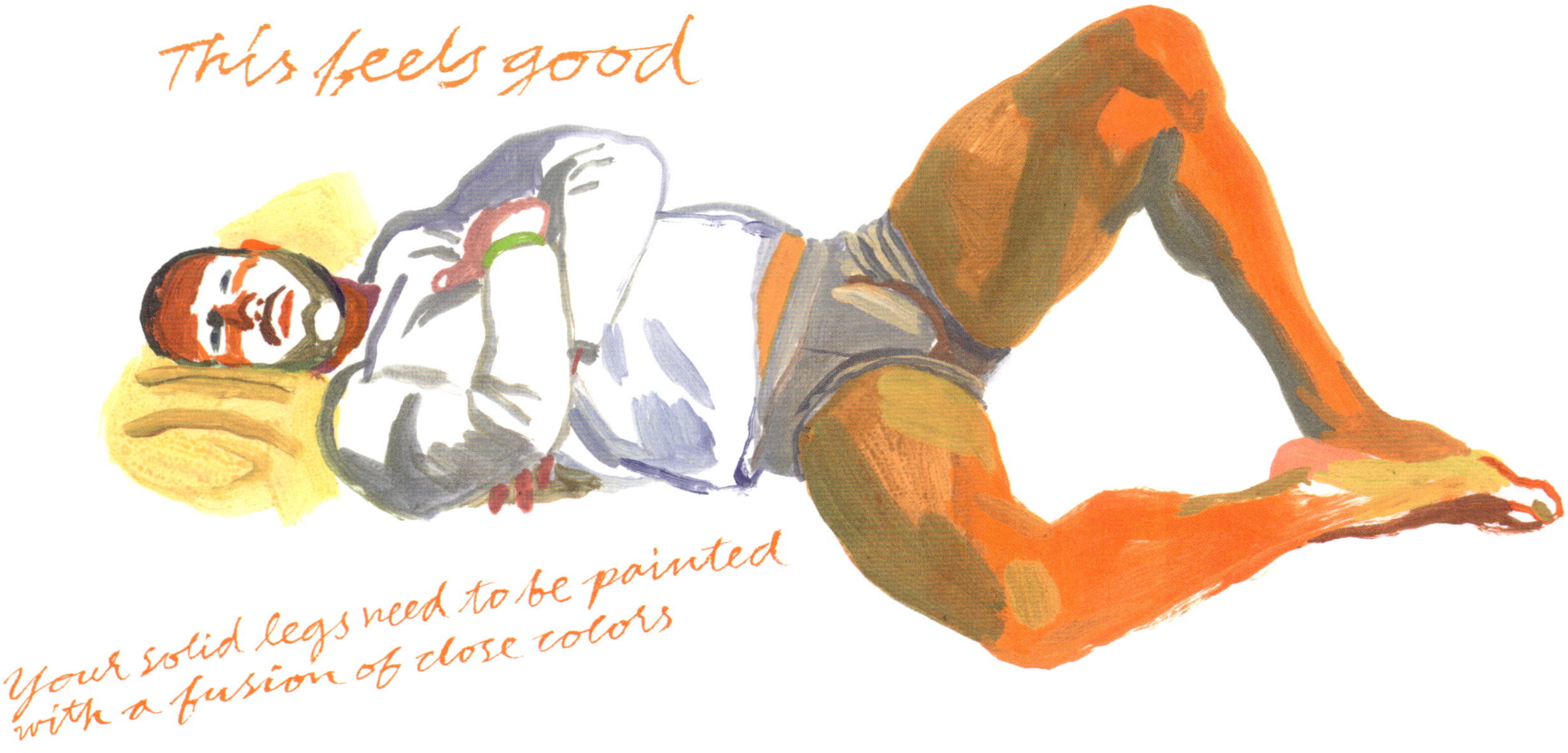
Your solid legs need to be painted with a fusion of close colors
I feel like I'm projecting into the future
Bracing forearm sets up looking-ahead face

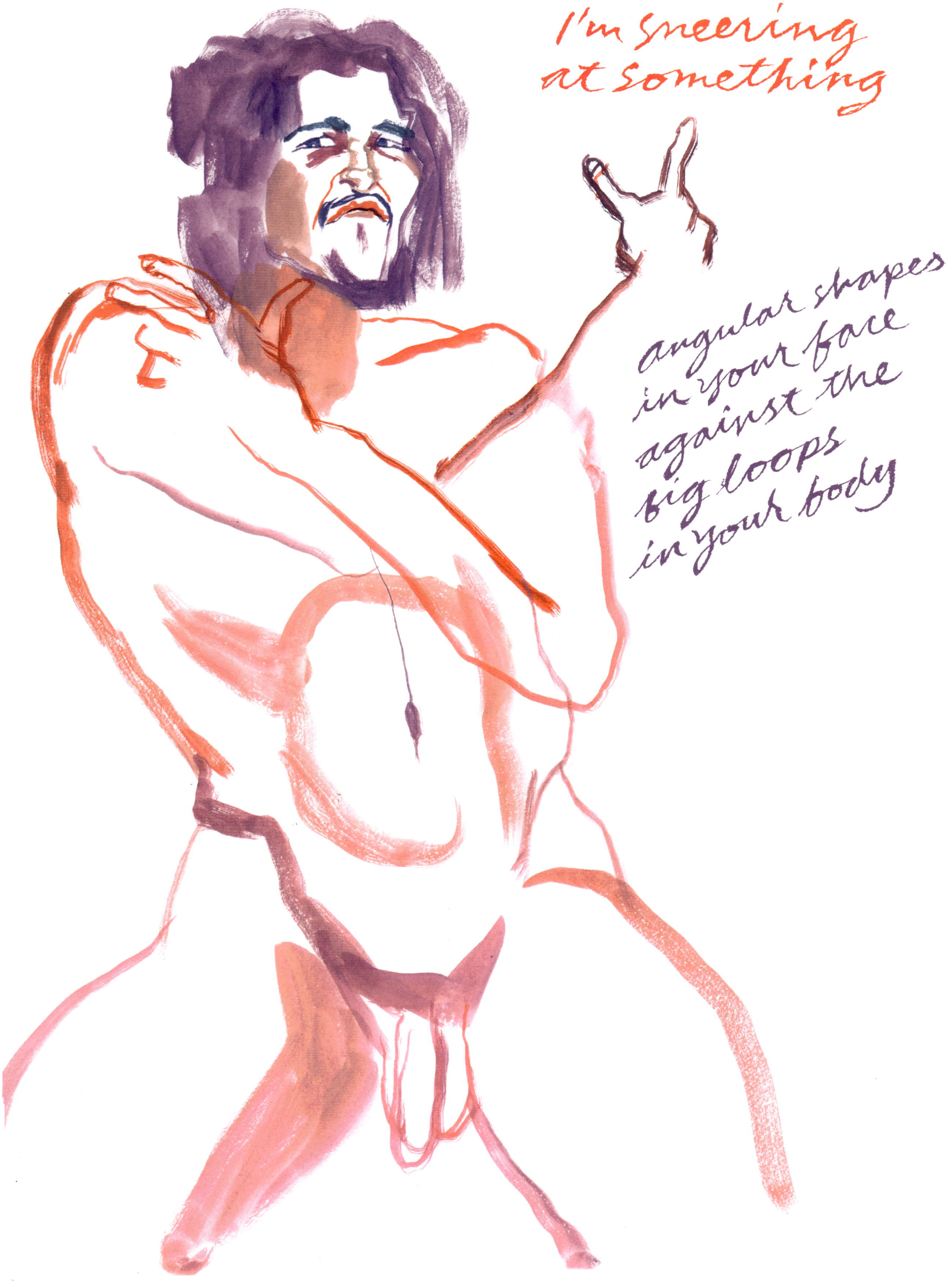

I'm sneering
at something

angular shapes
in your face
against the
big loops
in your body

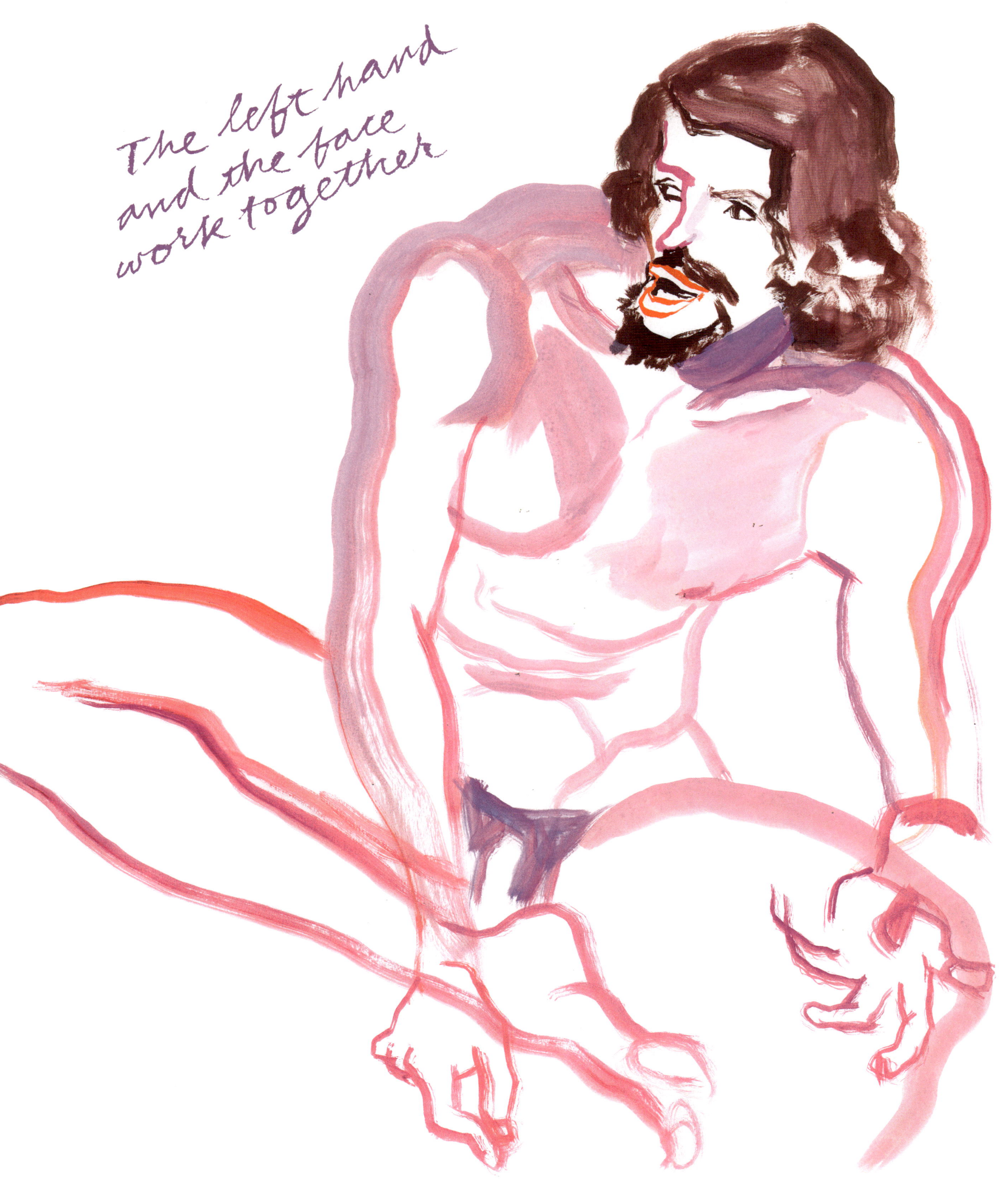
People are so hard
to convince

The left hand
and the face
work together

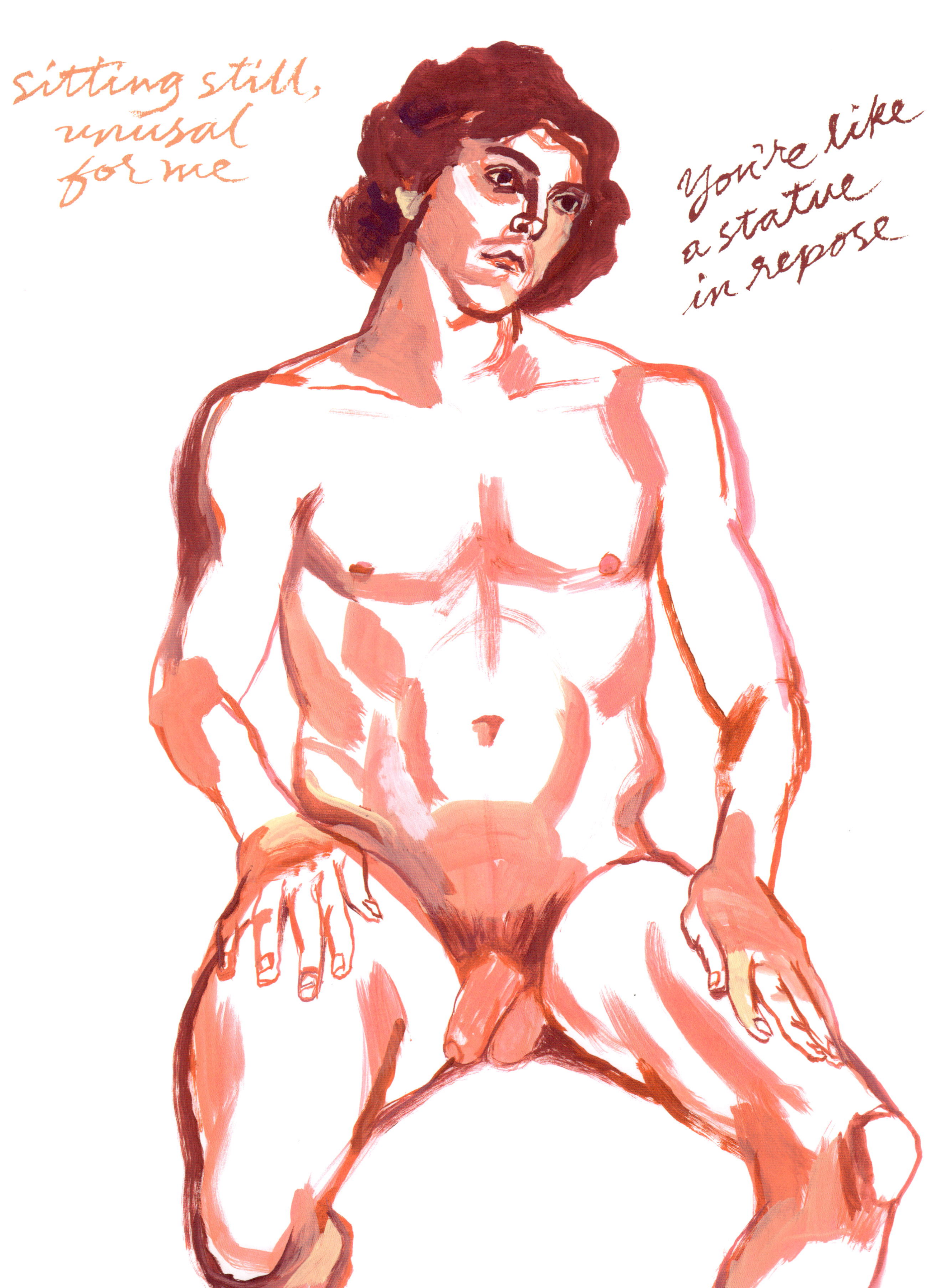
sitting still,
unusal
for me
You're like
a statue
in repose

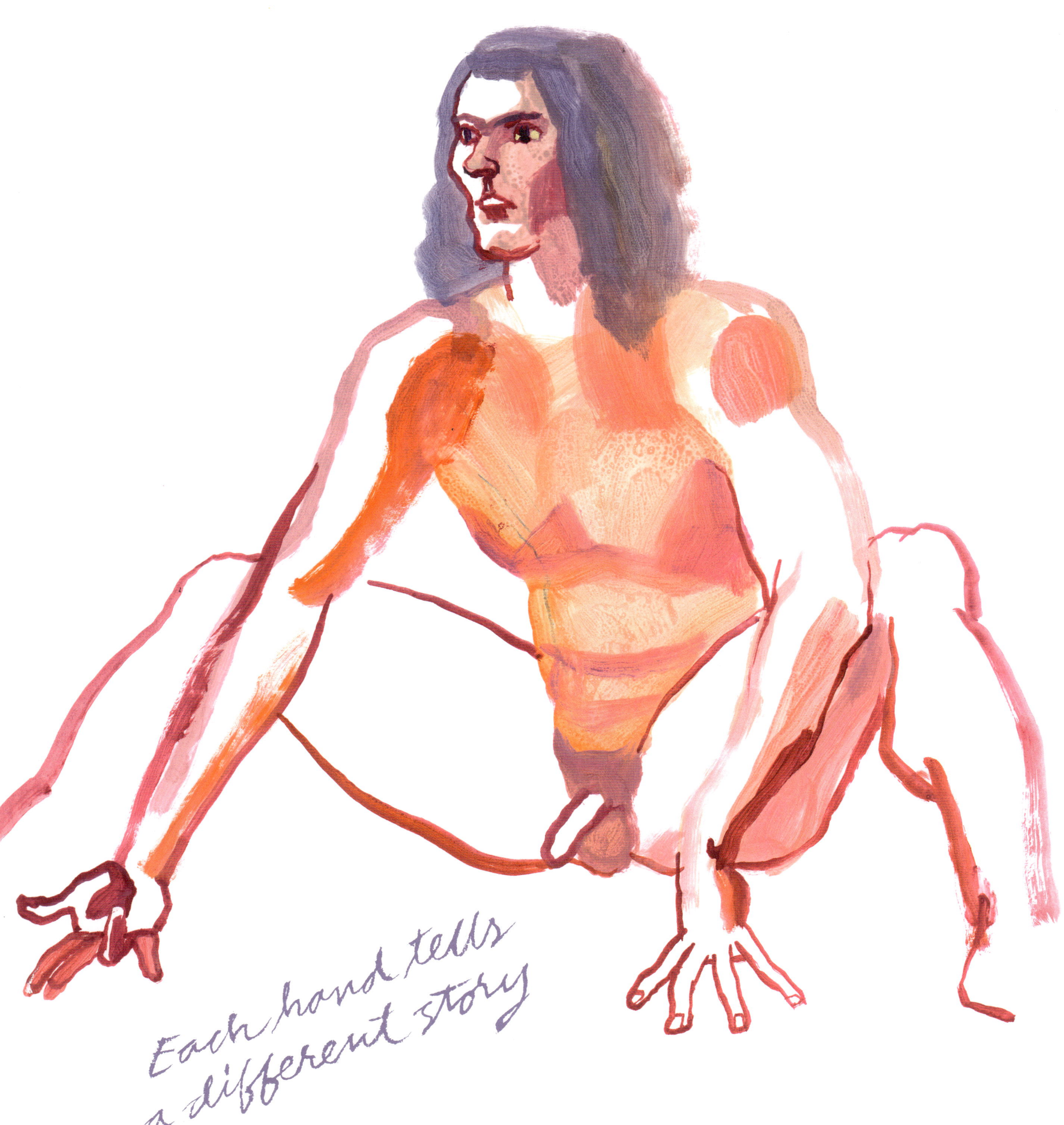I'm open to that
Each hand tells a different story

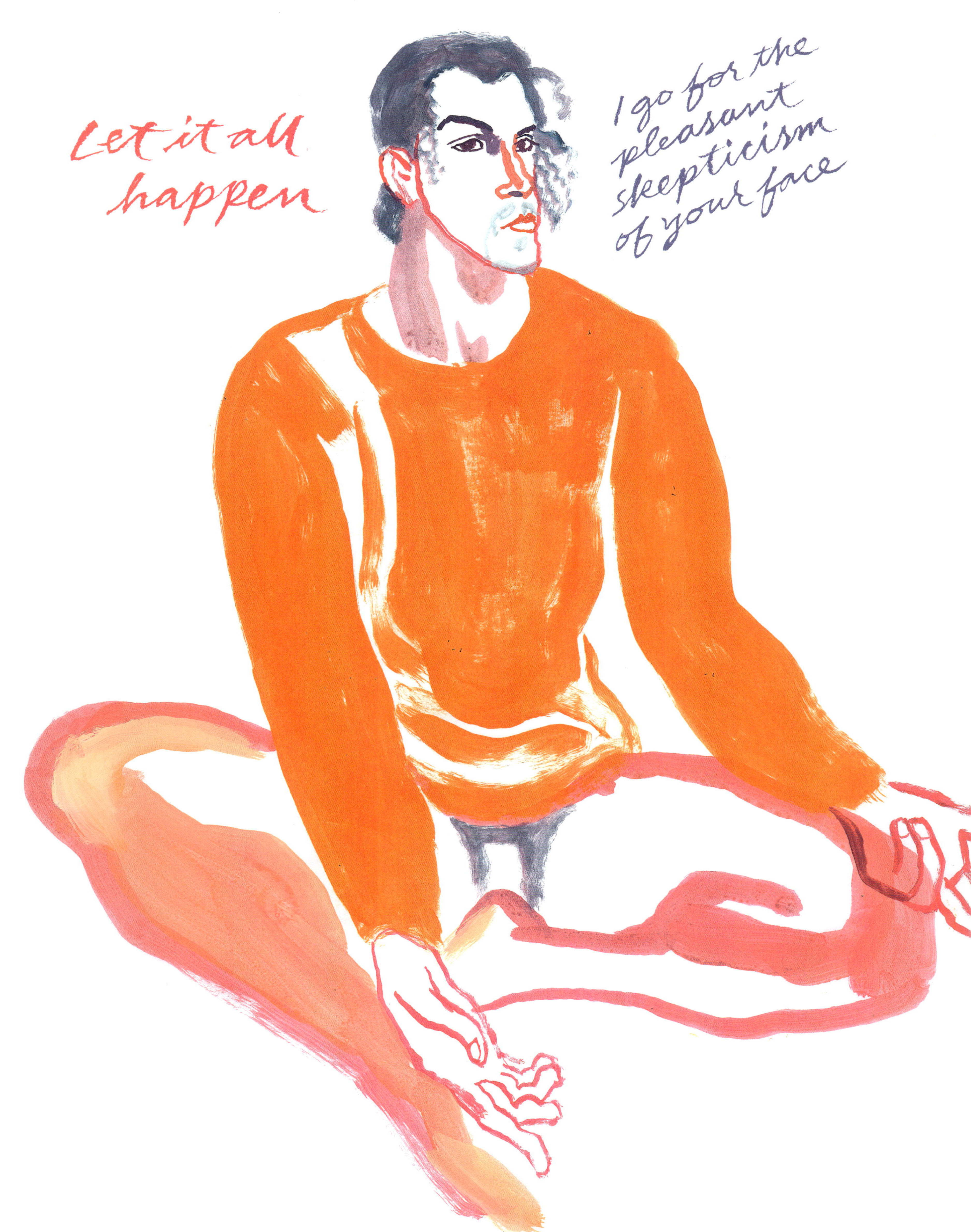

Let it all happen
I go for the pleasant skepticism of your face

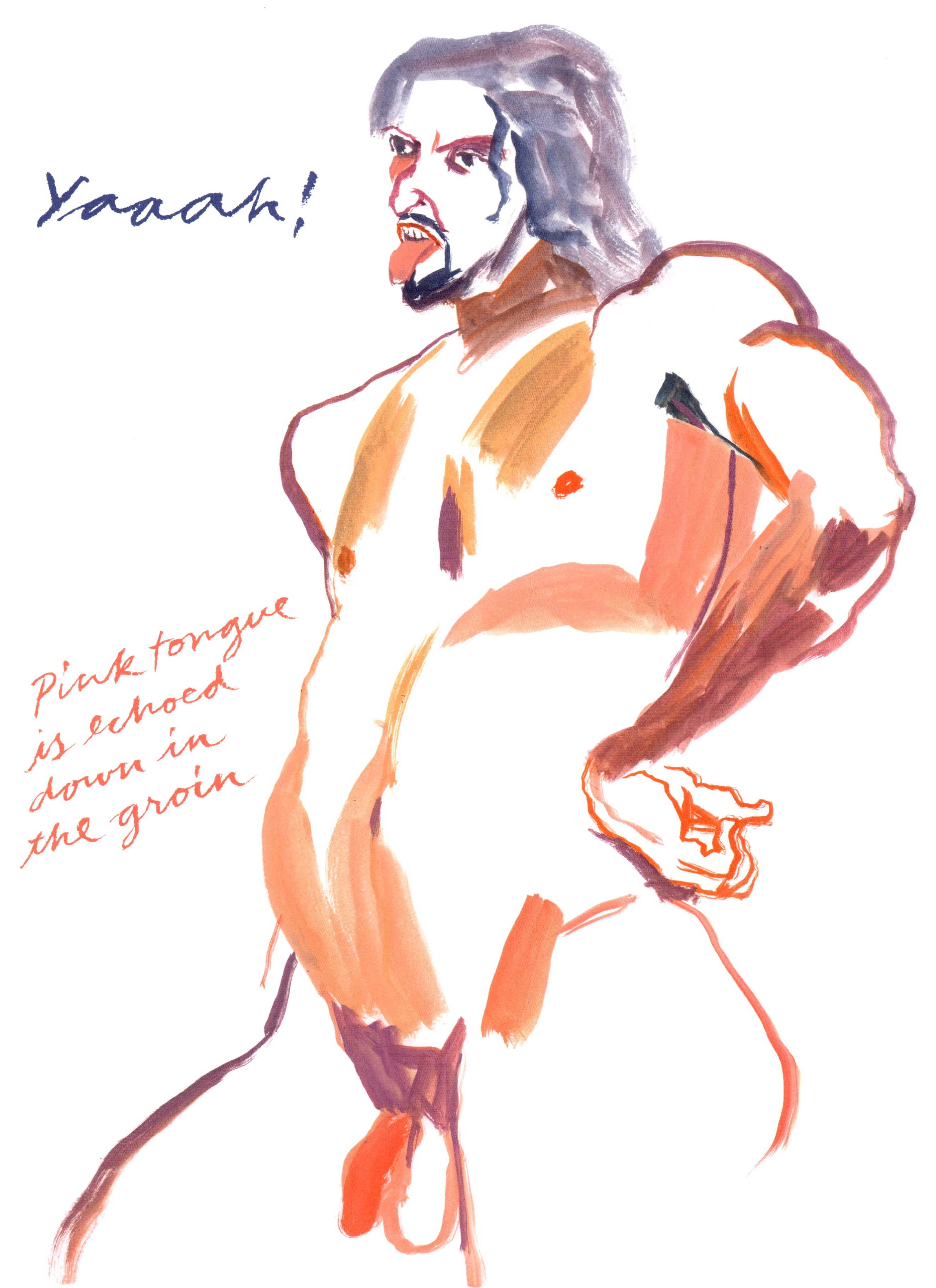

Yaaah!
Pink tongue
is echoed
down in
the groin

Yelling
from my
butt 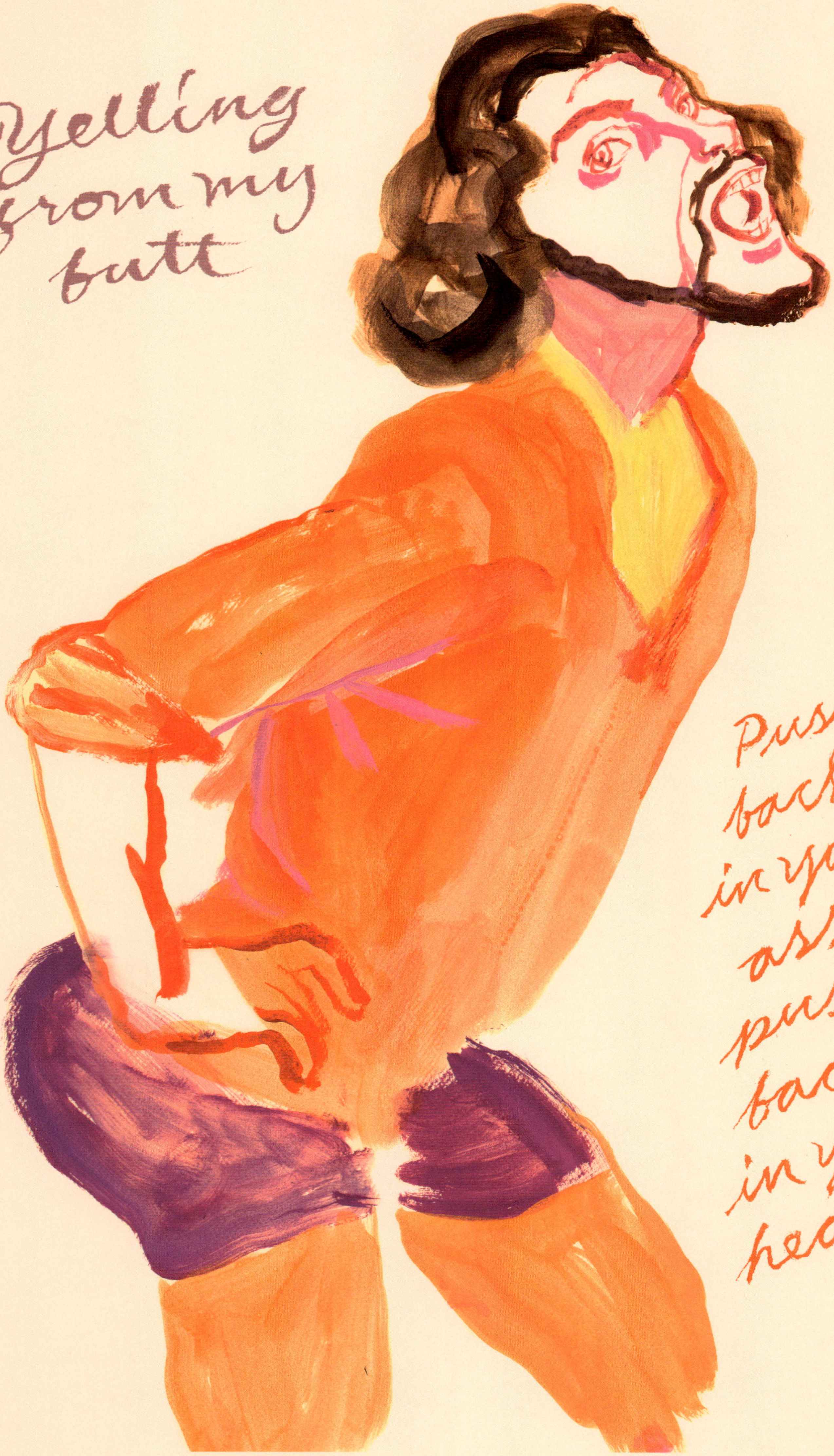
Push
back
in your
ass,
push
back
in your
head

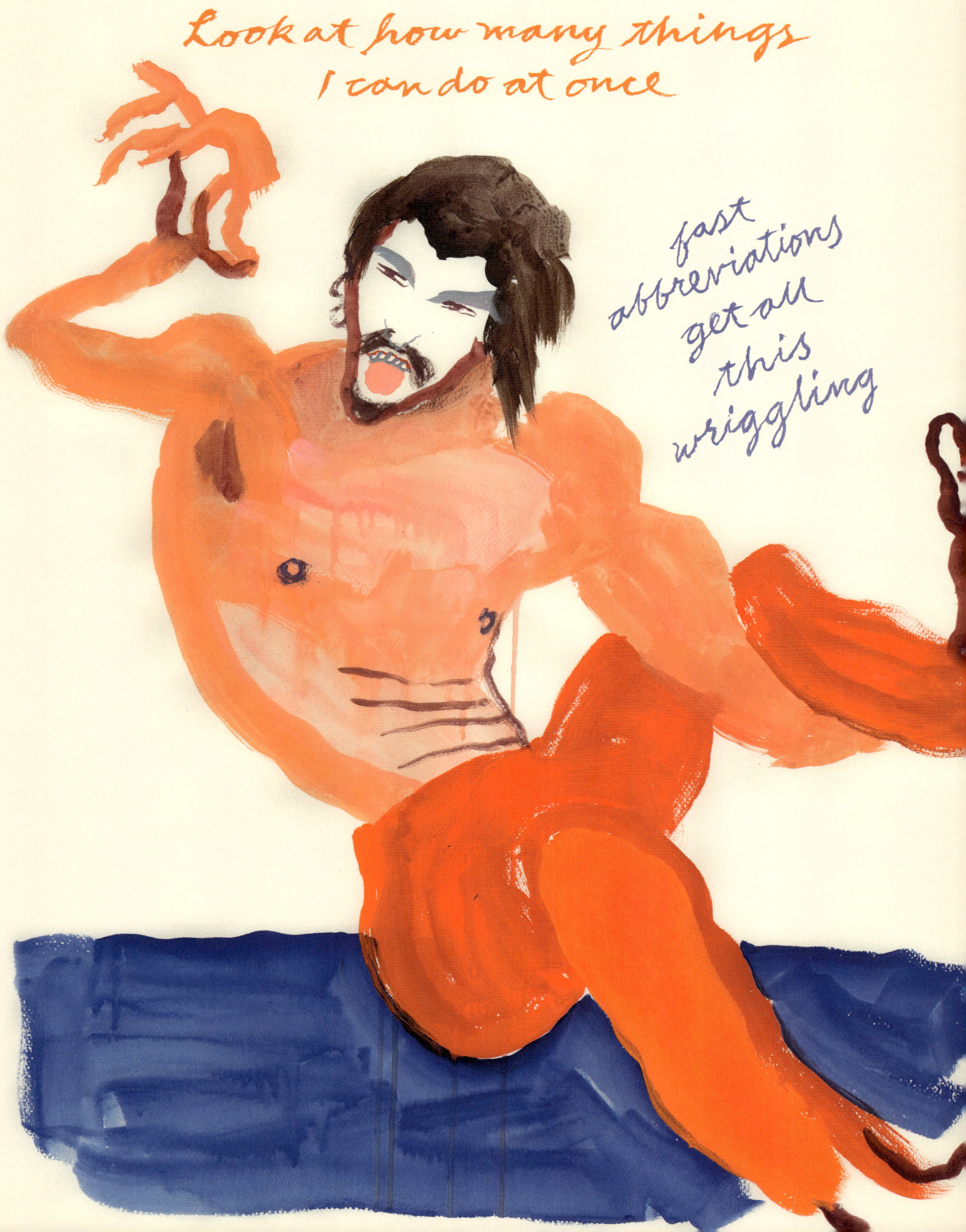

Look at how many things
I can do at once
fast
abbreviations
get all
this
wriggling

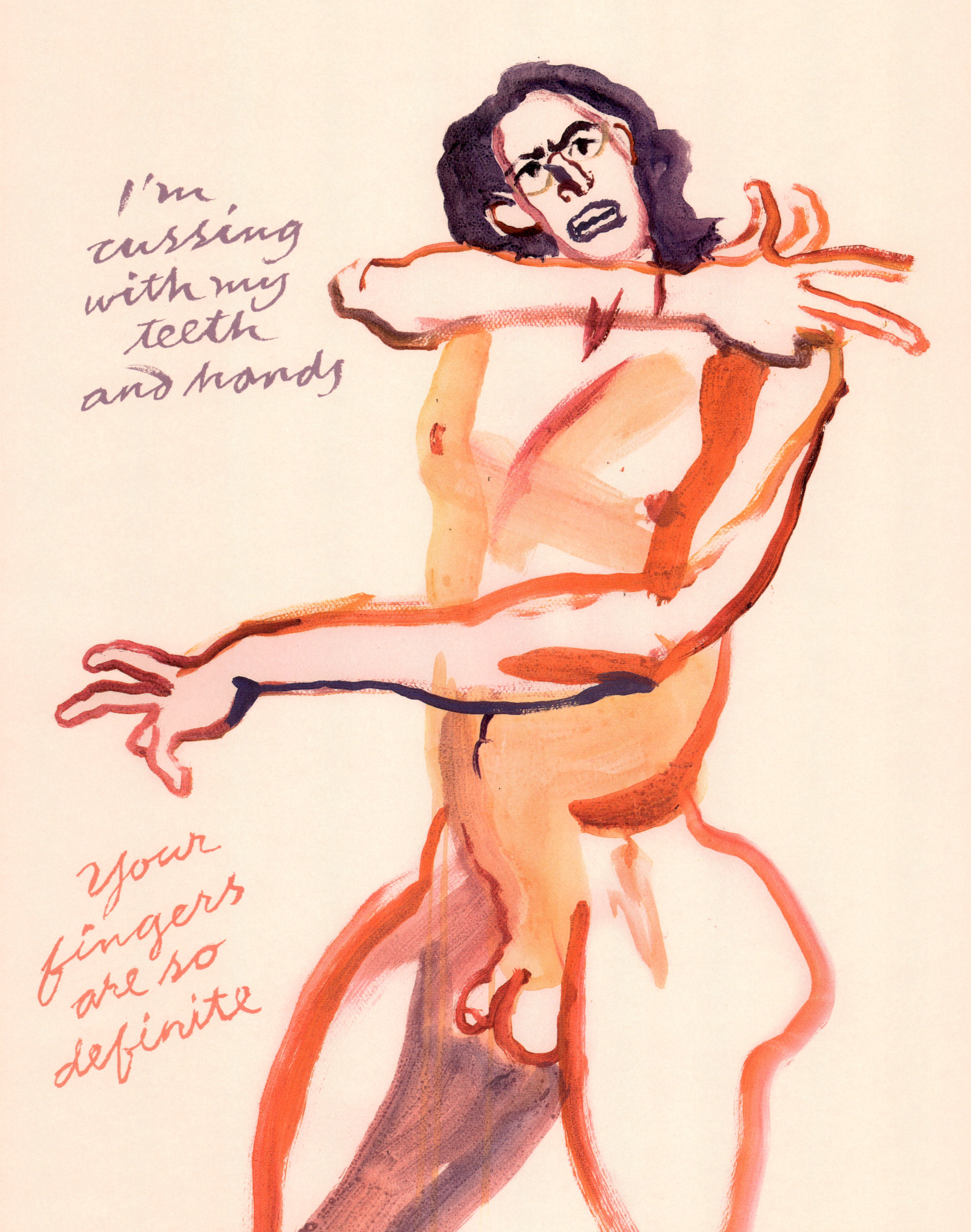

I'm
cussing
with my
teeth
and hands

Your
fingers
are so
definite

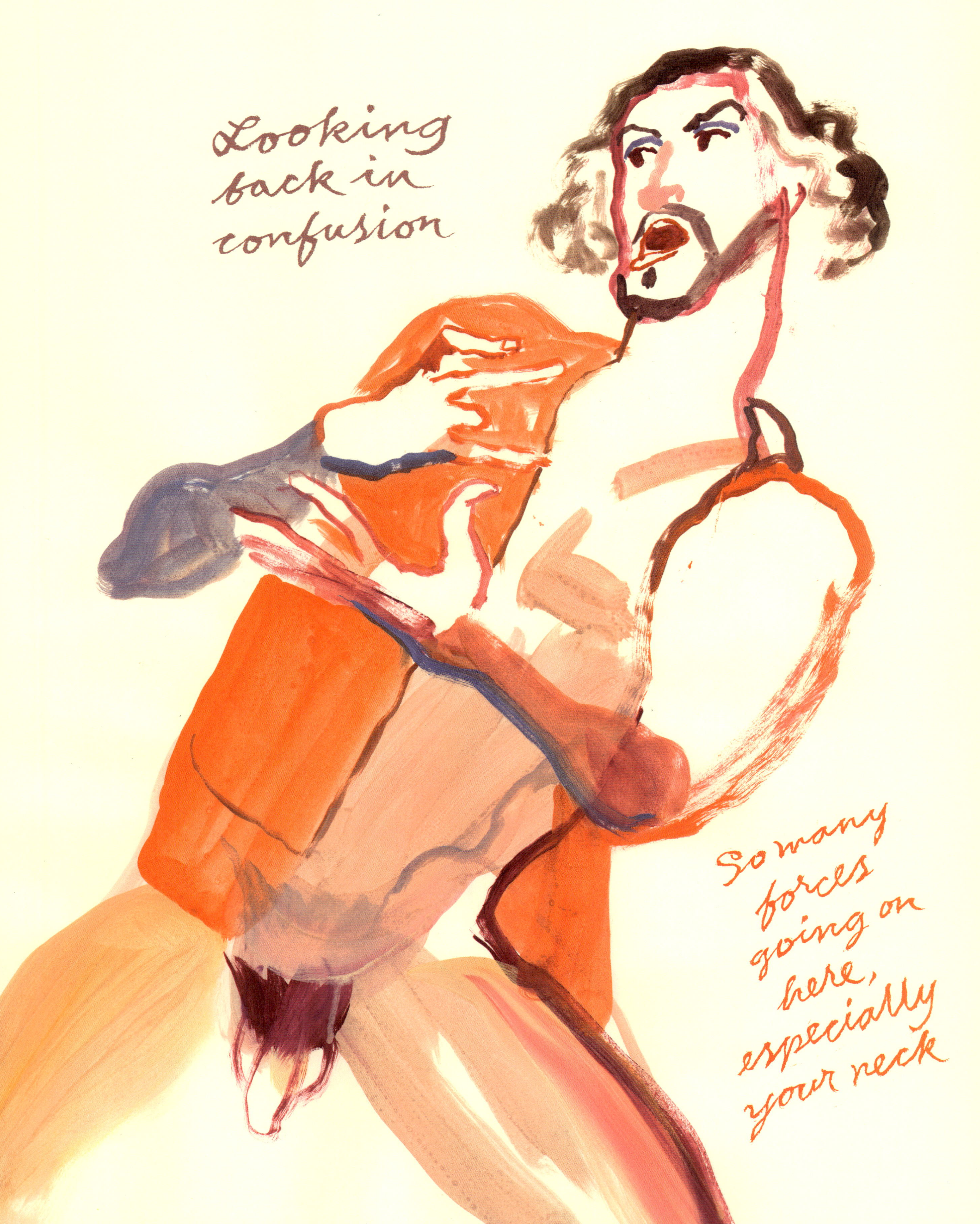
Looking back in confusion

So many forces going on here, especially your neck

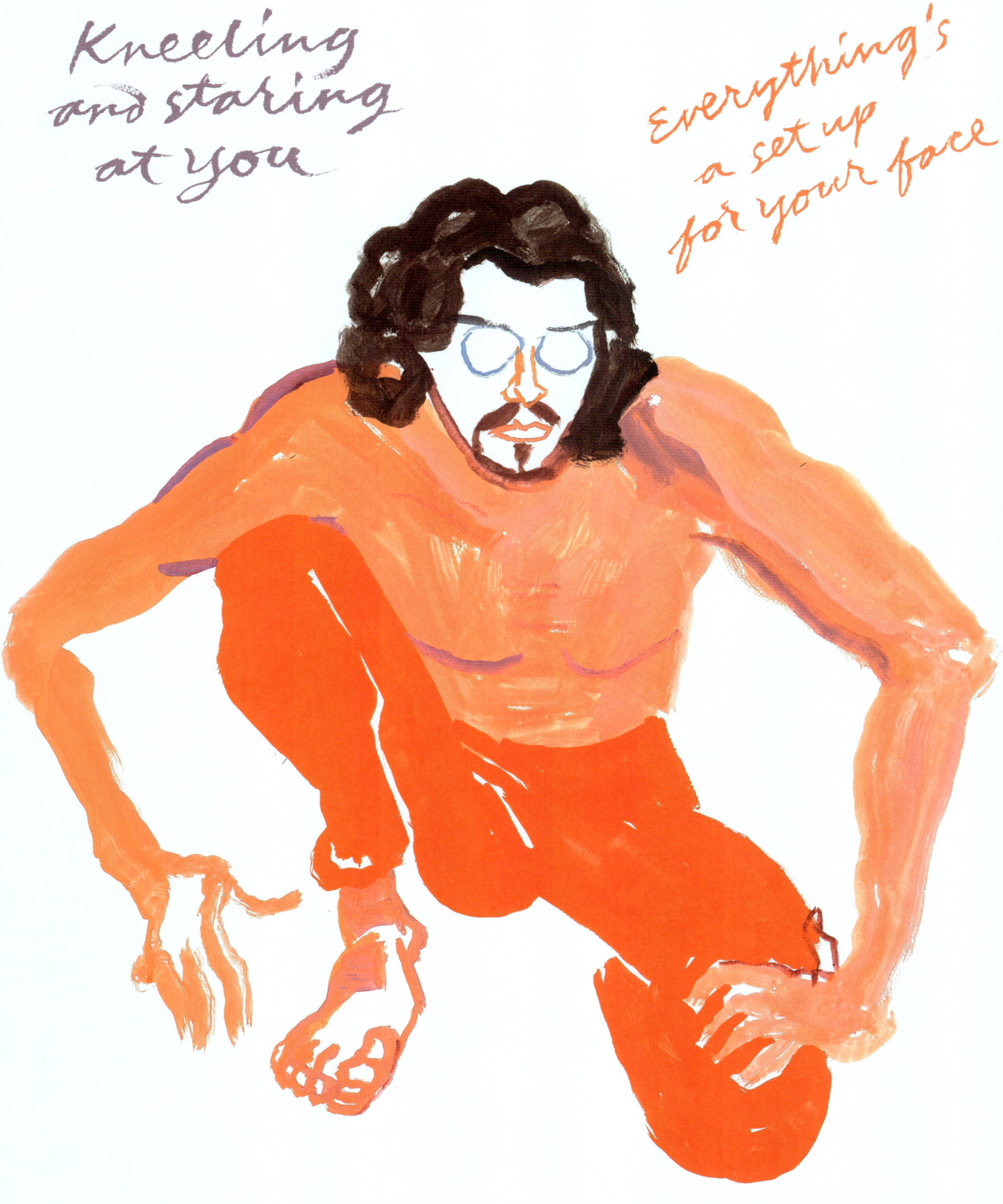

Kneeling
and staring
at you
Everything's
a set up
for your face

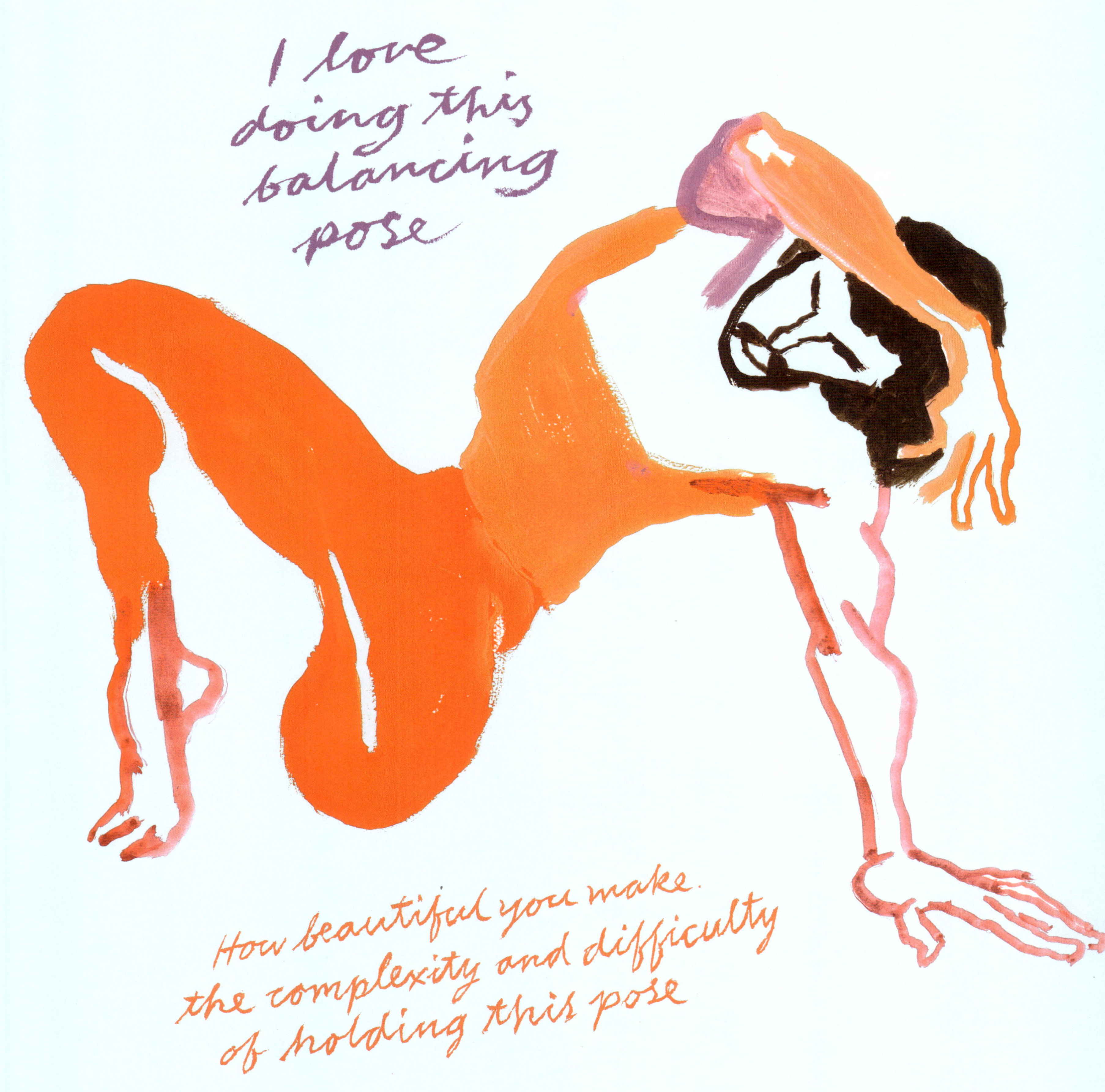

I love
doing this
balancing
pose

How beautiful you make
the complexity and difficulty
of holding this pose

I have
to leave now

The
questioning
intelligence
in your face
leads
everything

Conclusion

The timer dings.
The model relaxes and
steps off the stand.
Has my drawing taken me
to that intense place where I
saw and felt something I had
never seen or felt before?
Did my energy make a
connection to his energy
in a way that is different
from any other drawing?

Did I draw a person
and not a model?

James McMullan's 90 posters for Lincoln Center Theater include Anything Goes, Carousel, The Front Page and My Fair Lady. His paintings of a Brooklyn Disco for New York magazine became the visual inspiration for the movie Saturday Night Fever.

With his wife Kate he has created many children's books including the perennial favorite, I Stink! His other books include Revealing Illustrations, The Theater Posters of James McMullan and the illustrated memoir of his WWII childhood, Leaving China. He has taught drawing at the School of Visual Arts in New York City for more than 20 years.

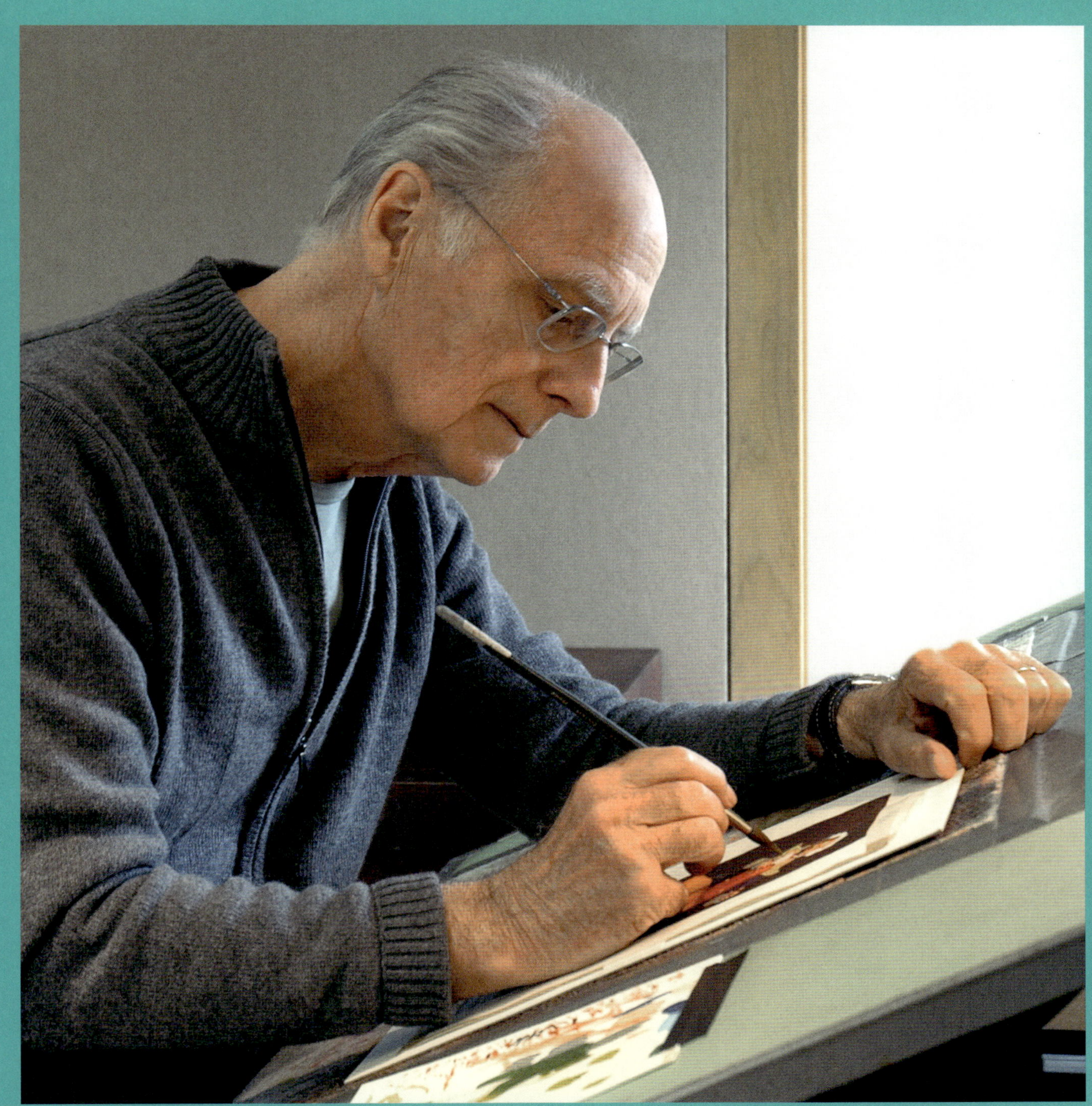

James McMullan

Acknowledgments

I thank:

Holly McGhee who challenged me to find the authentic spirit of the book. Suzanne Slesin and Frederico Farina who made the physical excellence of this book possible.

Peter Phobia who, beyond his irreplaceable skills on the computer, was my creative companion in helping me make the right choices in the book.

Publisher / Editorial Director **SUZANNE SLESIN**

Graphic Designer **PETER PHOBIA**

Editorial Assistant **JULIAN COSMA**

ISBN: 978-1-938461-49-1 / Library of Congress number: 2022908199

Printed in Spain / First Edition